UNLIKELY FINISHER

BY DALE PETELINSEK

This book is dedicated to those who encourage others to take the first step, congratulate them in taking the last step, and most importantly drive them to constantly just keep taking the next step.

Cataloging-in-Publication data is available from the Library of Congress
ISBN-13: 978-1481969604
ISBN-10: 1481969609

FOREWORD

A week after my wife Kathy and I finished the 2010 IRONMAN®
Wisconsin, I had lunch with an old friend. I had not seen her in
almost a year and could not wait to tell her about completing the
race. After the small talk cleared, she told me that her breast cancer had reoccurred and she had undergone a mastectomy since
we had last talked.

She walked me through the financial and career problems
that arose from spending weeks away from work. She talked
about the impact on her family, losing her hair, and how hard it
had been to get up in the morning. She also discussed chemo-
therapy and the fear of another reoccurrence.

I was riveted by her story and asked question after question
about the ordeal. Her intestinal fortitude was impressive, and the
heroics of being a cancer survivor were truly amazing. Oddly, I
didn't have sympathy, but only absolute awe as she talked about
overcoming one horrific situation after another.

My story of the seventeen-hour triathlon race really didn't
belong in the same conversation, at that table, on that day. Her
story of struggle and sacrifice just to stay alive was so much
greater than my struggle of inconvenience and bravado just to
get an IRONMAN Wisconsin finisher's medal. I was completely
humbled at that moment. The gravity of my achievement was
placed into context.

When it was my turn to talk, I decided to tell her about the race anyway. About all the training, people, places, and experiences that make the 140.6-mile race what it is. About the sweat, blood, and tears of grown men and women who could not go any further. About the man with the smashed jaw and bleeding face, five miles from the finish line of the marathon, moving forward just one small step at a time.

About the woman who could not go more than a quarter-mile at a time without vomiting, who crossed the finish line ten minutes before the race cut-off time, then collapsed and was carried to the medical tent. About the 250-pound guy lying on the grass, his legs too cramped to move anymore, who was removed from the marathon because he would not make the projected finish cut-off. And about the complete and utter satisfaction I felt as I crossed the finish line.

This time she was oddly engaged, and we talked for quite some time. She seemed as interested in my story as I was in hers. I am not suggesting that there is any measure of equivalence, only a mutual appreciation of facing a challenge and beating the odds.

She was the first to mention that my story would make a good book. The suggestion was especially interesting coming from someone who had just under gone an event two orders of magnitude bigger than mine. I promised to send her a copy of the book if I ever took the time to write one.

Three years have passed since Kathy and I set out to run IRONMAN® Wisconsin. All of the literature we found when we first researched the event discussed only the winners and achievers. None of it was targeted at the average or, in my case, below-average athlete.

Last night I picked up a new *Triathlon magazine*, and the headlines advertised a report of some professional athlete's thoughts after winning a big race. Inside the magazine, all of the advertisements showed professional athletes or models pimping the latest go-fast gear. What a bunch of BS. Most of the people I met during the two years we spent preparing for the race just talked about what it takes to finish. Only one person is going to win the race. The rest of us come in after that. Me, I come in much closer to last than to first. What about us? Who writes a book from the perspective of the back of the pack? What literature is written for the finisher rather than the winner?

This book is written for the guy who has no idea when he begins training if he will actually make it to the starting line on race day, much less make it to the finish. This book is written for the white-collar desk jockey who can't acclimatize to the heat because he sits in an air-conditioned office all day.

This book is written for the full-time parent who can't train all weekend because she has children to feed and bills to pay. This book is written for the fifty-year-old guy who likes to take a weekend off from training and go out binge drinking and cigar smoking because hanging out with kids who wear spandex, eat right, train often, and live in their parents' basements is only so much fun.

The events that I have recorded in this book are real. In some areas, I have grouped together events or combined a couple of people into a single character to make the book more readable. I have changed some names. Of course, different people's perspectives on a single event can vary greatly. I have tried to talk to the people involved and get their feedback, but I am sure that I have missed several thoughts and perspectives in putting this together.

My sincere hope is that this book will inspire you to try the extraordinary, to beat the odds, to take a chance and cross the finish line on your feet, then fall on your back and shout out to God just how damn glad you are to be alive!

Maybe, just maybe, this book will inspire you to go out and run a mile. Who knows, you may work up to running 26.2 miles after finishing a 112-mile bike ride and a 2.4-mile swim. I did it, and there is no more unlikely IRONMAN® athlete than myself. My wife did it, and ten years ago she could not even run a mile. So sit back, flip open the first chapter of this book, and dig in. It was eighteen months of intense training followed by one very long day on the course.

Semper Fidelis
Dale "The Possum" Petelinsek

Decision

Every time I retell the story, I remember more clearly how the sun rose in the north woods early that morning. The towering jack pines and numerous aspens were perfectly still. A pair of grouse had already left their roost and were stretching their legs and pecking the sandy ground. Perfect and complete silence. A grey jay swooped down to a branch in front of the cabin window as the sunshine peaking through the trees slowly evaporated the early fall frost into a light haze.

Light began to filter into the hunting lodge's great room as the sun rose over the trees. I watched dust particles float up and dance in the air. A heavy silence filled the cabin, aside from the occasional snore or cough from the bunks in the basement.

The lodge was 4000 square feet of log cabin man heaven. Real hand cut logs stacked into tall walls. Antlers, skins, traps, and guns tacked up with rusty nails. Beer signs, billiards, ping-pong, and foosball on the three-season porch. A cast-iron barrel stove giving off a smoldering heat.

Inside, the air was still filled with the previous night's cigar smoke. Empty cans and bottles, overfilled ashtrays, and the remains of the last hand of poker were strewn about the kitchen table.

Just outside the patio door, hundreds of spent shell casings cluttered the deck. Beer cans and liquor bottles were everywhere, some still intact, most with bullet holes in them. The musty smell of eight guys, two dogs, and outdoor plumbing clung to anything that was upholstered.

Since I was up early that day, I poured a little rum in my coffee cup and then a bigger amount in my friend Nate's. Nate, also awake, was cooking breakfast. His breakfast was deer camp legend consisting of eggs, bacon, potatoes, and french toast. The clanging of pots and pans shot through my ears and spiked into my head. I hoped that a few aspirins mixed with the rum and coffee would cure the immense hangover that had me in its tight grip.

I lit the first smoke of the day, coughed, and pushed open the kitchen door to spit outside. The old wooden screen door creaked as it opened and crashed as it slammed back shut. I finished my cup of java and poured the second with even more rum. We sat down for bacon and eggs.

The day's goal was to cut shooting lanes into the thick forest, improving our chances of harvesting deer from our tree stands later that year. We never quite knew what we would need for an adventure in the north woods, so we packed heavy. That day we loaded cigars, chewing tobacco, the rest of the rum, gasoline, chain saws, long arms, and hand guns onto our four-wheel-drive ATVs. The four-wheelers were splattered with mud and beer from the late-night ride that had ended just a few hours ago. We turned the motors over and spun off into the wild.

We returned for lunch four hours later, empty-handed and tumbling drunk.

We sat down at the kitchen table, took off our boots, and started talking smart. Smart like you can only do after killing a fifth of rum before noon on a Saturday. I love day drinking, and as is often said, you can't say you drank all day unless you started early in the morning. This place, this lifestyle, was my identity—hunting deer, drinking beer, and smoking cigars with my friends was my true passion.

After lunch and a brief nap, we piled into my pickup truck. The tires spun small swirls of frosted autumn leaves into the air as we fishtailed down the long road into town. Nate vomited the morning's rum onto the floor of my truck. Back in cell phone range, my ringer went off. It was my wife, Kathy.

Volunteer

I pulled the truck over to the side of the road and stepped out. The two-lane highway was straight, long, and empty. Crystal clear water stood in small puddles on the ground. I climbed to the top of a moss-covered granite boulder nearby. By leaning slightly to the left I could get just enough bars on my cell phone to hear Kath's sweet voice over the silence of the north woods.

Things at home were fine, and Kathy said that she was doing research on the Internet about the IRONMAN® Wisconsin race. We had been talking about the 140.6-mile triathlon for a few weeks already. Our talk consisted mostly of her bringing it up and me saying that I could never and would never do the race. After a few minutes she would say that she wanted to do the race, and then the subject would drop.

Kath told me that she wanted to register us as volunteer workers for the upcoming race. The phone was silent for a minute as she waited for my approval. A red squirrel ran across the pine needles and headed up a tree. He looked down from a branch over my head and scolded me in heavy chirps and barks. Nate was done vomiting and began honking the horn so we could get going. A moth flew by my head, too stubborn or too stupid to know that it would freeze to death as soon as the sun went down. I was having trouble focusing, my hands were getting cold, I needed a drink, and my attention was running short.

I told Kath again that I was not interested in running a full distance triathlon. She asked me if it was okay for the two of us to volunteer and just see what the race was about. She said that after we volunteered, we could make up our minds about running the race the following year. I told her a second time that I was not interested in running IRONMAN® Wisconsin, but I would volunteer. She was so excited that she went online to sign us up while I was still on the phone.

My hands were a little shaky, so I lit another cigarette to calm myself down after the conversation. I took a deep drag and let the smoke linger in my lungs then slowly exhaled rings into the still air. The unnatural stress of a countdown clock starting off in the distance registered in my subconscious. I knew that volunteering would eventually lead to running that race. With the tick tock of the training clock now ringing in the back of my brain, I piled back in the truck with Nate and drove to the bar.

I remember drinking Jägermeister and Red Bull shots that afternoon. This would be my last binge for the year—I wanted it to be a good one.

Kathy

Kathy is an endurance machine. At 5'7" and 120 pounds, with huge swimmer's shoulders and a small runner's tail, she is what every man dreams about and every woman wants to be. Her platinum blonde hair, blue eyes, and dimpled smile make her easy on the eyes. Her personality and charm make her a keeper. Her unnatural desire to be first at whatever she does makes her annoying to be around at times—especially when competing. They say that fives don't marry tens, but I certainly got the best of this marriage.

Kath didn't start running until she was in her late thirties. She started by running no further than one mailbox down the country road from our house, about a quarter of a mile, then turning around and running back. Then she went two mailboxes, then to the white mailbox by the barking dog, a full mile. She completed a marathon during her second year as a runner. In her third year she did two marathons, and in her fourth year she did four. Now in her mid-forties, she had finished a dozen marathons and two half-distance triathlons.

Whether running a business, raising kids or decorating a cake, Kath is constantly pushing further and striving to be the best at everything she tries.

A Little About Me

I did not grow up an athlete. I never carried the football across the goal line the last game of my senior year of high school. Neither was I an academic. In fact, I was pretty far removed from the high school honor roll. As a youngster I focused on drinking beer with close friends, hunting on cold mornings, fishing on hot days, souped-up motorcycles, snow skiing, fist fights, rock and roll, tobacco, muscle cars, and pretty girls, probably in that order. Organized sports was at best a distraction from the things I truly enjoyed.

As the result of a minor infraction with the law, I ended up in the Marine Corps at a young age. This helped me escape the reality of the life I was heading toward. The Corps taught me about honor, discipline, execution, and leadership. These are things I value today and hope that I instill in the people around me.

They say that the A students in high school end up working for the B students and the C students own the companies that both the A and B students are employed at. I was a C student in high school and college. I started my first computer software company in 1996 and have not looked back since. Fifteen years later, I have added real estate and farming operations to our family's portfolio.

I began distance running while I was in the Marine Corps, mostly as a way to clear my head from the immense hangovers we would rack up after a hard night on the town. Years later, I kept running for fun and to keep my body lean and my mind strong.

Some people golf during their free time. I go out for runs with my family, my friends, my dog, or even by myself if no one else is around. By 2009 I had completed ten marathons. None were finished in competitive times, but all came with a sense of camaraderie and accomplishment that those types of adventures bring.

As you read further along in this book, I don't want to send the message that I or my friends and family are binge drinking, cigar smoking, knock down drag out hell raisers. Truth be told, though, we do have our moments.

The Team

A few weeks ago, Kathy and I were introduced as "the couple who does marathons and stuff." Of all of the things that we have done in our life, this is the last one that I thought we would be recognized for. Kath and I met in high school and have been together pretty much since then. We have raised kids, cats, poultry, livestock and even a squirrel named Rocky. We stay active in the church, our community, and our professional circles. Actually, up to this point, I would never have thought that we would even be recognized as joggers.

I was told early on that it can put a huge amount of stress on a marriage if only one person is training for such a grueling race. I think that this is an understatement. Because all you really do for a year is train, sleep, or work, I don't know how you would ever keep in touch with your spouse if you were not training with him or her.

According to my daughter Anna, Kathy and I have sworn after every triathlon we have done that we would never do another. That is what made my wife's fascination with doing this race, the triathlon of triathlons, seem curious to me.

Driving to Volunteer at 2009 IRONMAN® Wisconsin

The first weekend in September 2009, Kathy and I packed up the car and drove 281 miles from our home in Minneapolis to Madison. Our youngest daughter was a freshman at the University of Wisconsin that year, so the trip had a dual purpose. We could both visit her and volunteer at the triathlon.

The IRONMAN brand is to triathlon what the Super Bowl is to pee-wee football. The point of the race is to finish a 140.6-mile course within a firm cut-off time of seventeen hours. In this time, you swim 2.4 miles, bike 112 miles, and then run a 26.2-mile marathon. As if the shear distance isn't enough, the swim is done in open water with 2500 athletes all climbing on top of each other as they compete to swim the shortest line. The bike portion is done on the most severe elevations. Almost every mile is either straight up or straight down, and if the swimming and cycling don't kill you, the full marathon at the end just might.

The biggest variable in a long-distance triathlon is not the course, the equipment, or the athlete; it is the weather. Winds over 15 miles per hour will kick up waves and make the 2.4-mile swim a life or death survival slosh. Winds over 20 miles per hour will make the 112-mile bike race a thigh buster. Conversely, a lack of wind can make a runner feel like he is baking in a convection oven if the temperature climbs above 75° F.

The sun can also have a huge effect. A sunny 90° F day can make it uncomfortable for a spectator to stand and watch the race for a few hours. This same temperature will send an unprepared athlete into the medical tent for an IV and an early trip home.

Cold weather can drain a competitor of their body fluids and cause hypothermia. A race day rain can make for slippery roads and blistered feet. Nature sure can be a "mother" to the competitor.

If the first four horses of the triathlete's apocalypse are wind, heat, cold, and rain, the fifth is humidity. Humidity draws the fluids out of an athlete faster than they can consume them and leaves the unprepared crashed on the course in a sweaty slump.

My wife feared cold weather and rain; I feared the warm temperatures and high humidity that can occur during September in Wisconsin.

The uninitiated who do not understand the significance of the long-distance triathlon often confuse it with the shorter Sprint triathlon (nineteen-mile) or Olympic triathlon (thirty-one-mile). I also hear it confused with Century bike rides (100 miles) and marathons (26.2 miles). It is only after you explain that an IRONMAN® event is further than a Century ride and a marathon put together that people start to grasp the significance.

The IRONMAN series of triathlons started in the late 1970s and eventually became a brand with the enormous marketing engine and publicity that make it the spectacle it is today. There are 17 full distance IRONMAN-branded races and 34 half-distance IRONMAN® 70.3®-branded races each year. The race in Kailua-Kona, Hawaii is the world championship event for the IRONMAN® series. If you have never seen an IRONMAN event, I would suggest that you put this on your bucket list. If you already have completing in IRONMAN race on your bucket list, I would suggest that you reevaluate your list. It is truly a sport that you enter at your own risk.

The Madison course has a reputation for having the second-highest dropout rate and the second-slowest finishing times. This is due primarily to the extreme number and size of the hills on the bike course. I was unable to comprehend why anyone would want to do the IRONMAN Wisconsin race instead of a flatter course. We picked the location for one because we didn't know any better, and for two because it was close to our home in Minneapolis.

We got to the hotel the day before the race and walked into the lobby. Gear and athletes and food and empty packages were scattered everywhere. Athletes were walking around kind of quietly. Some were stretching, others were rushing about. Most seemed in a zombie-like daze, focused only on preparing for the next day. In every corner athletes were fumbling with gear. Some had the 1000-yard stare that comes with the anxiety surrounding a life-changing event. None of them looked me in the eyes. They just went about their tasks. There was something about the air in the hotel. You could tell that something big was about to happen the next day.

The élan or esprit of these IRONMAN athletes attracted me. I wanted to be one of the athletes. I wanted to feel some of the excitement they had. I wanted to be one of the badasses who could swim, bike, and run 140.6 miles. At that moment I really wanted to be an IRONMAN finisher.

Passing Out Water at Cross Plains Water Stop

We showed up to the small town of Cross Plains, Wisconsin, early the following morning. We met the fifty or so other volunteers we would work with handing out water to athletes. The Cross Plains water stop was located about 40 miles into the 112-mile bike course. The athletes would ride through this water stop twice in the two-loop course—the first time at forty miles, the second time at eighty.

The Madison bike course is laid out like a lollipop. It is roughly a sixteen-mile line out to a forty-mile loop. The riders ride out along the "stick," ride twice around the "lollipop" at the end, and then go back down the stick. The mile-long water stop was the only flat section of the 112-mile course of extreme ups and downs.

We started the day by removing bottles of water and Gatorade from container boxes and putting them into ice-filled inflatable pools. When an athlete came screaming past on a bike, we would hold up a water bottle and he or she would grab it on the fly while riding past.

Depending on the temperature and the course, an athlete can drink between twelve and twenty-four ounces of water per hour.

A bike usually holds two to four bottles of water on board, so this water refueling station was a welcome sight for thirsty athletes. Water is not only used for drinking. Athletes also squirt it on their heads to cool down.

I could not help but get caught up in the excitement of the day as the riders flew past. What a sight! I met a few volunteers who had actually finished the race in previous years, and I could not help but be in awe of their accomplishment. Oddly, one thing I noticed about them was just how out of shape they looked now. They had very little muscle tone, bellies hung over their waistbands, their shoulders were slumped. It was like they just let themselves go after the race.

As the current year's athletes whizzed past, I felt the pure shock and awe that I had traditionally reserved for rock stars and guys who had shot monster deer. They were trim, ripped, and eagle-eyed. All of them focused on laying it down on the course and getting across the finish line in a competitive time.

State Street

After our shift was up at the water stop, we decided to drive into Madison to watch the athletes run the marathon. On the drive into town we called my daughter Anna, who left the college and met us on the State Street mall in downtown Madison. State Street is a classic off-campus, Big Ten pedestrian mall that, in true Wisconsin fashion, has a bar about every 100 feet. The mall is typically filled with a mix of students, homeless people, state workers, and street performers. Today the entertainment was the run segment of this IRONMAN® race, a full marathon. The first and last mile of each loop ran up and down this street, making it a great place to get a beer and watch the race.

We sat down under the shade of an umbrella and ordered Long Island iced teas. The athletes passed just two feet from us on the other side of the cattle grates that outlined the course. While they were locked in a struggle to take each step, here we were getting plowed on foo-foo cocktails. Not many people could recognize the huge difference between us and the athletes. I did, and the juxtaposition was not lost on me.

A friend of Kathy's from high school joined us out on the patio. He had done IRONMAN Wisconsin the year before and was also volunteering that day. I tried to pry into his psyche to understand why he had chosen to take on this most grueling adventure.

He said two things. First, he said that hundreds of thousands of people can say that they have run a marathon, but only a fraction of those can say that they have completed an IRONMAN® race.

Second, when we questioned him about the amount of time we were projecting to spend training, he said that yes, all an athlete does is eat, sleep, and train for an entire year. He went on further to say that yes, you will lose all of your social connections in that year. But really, you are only losing a year of your life to gain this huge accomplishment. In his opinion, it was well worth it.

We sat for few hours while the sun set on the horizon. I looked deep into the faces of the runners passing by to see if I had what they did—the strength to finish an IRONMAN triathlon. As the day slipped away, we walked past the state capitol back to our car. Here, the faster runners were finishing their second loop of the marathon and the slower runners were just getting off their bikes to begin the first loop.

We watched the first female finisher cross the finish line. There was a lot of fanfare, and a camera crew closed in on her for an interview. She looked skeleton-skinny and was as white as ghost, but otherwise was quite composed for someone who just swam, biked, and ran 140.6 miles.

We walked past her, and when I crossed the course I almost ran into a fifty-something man who had just gotten off his bike and was starting the run. He was a big guy like myself, maybe 6'4" and 230 pounds. In triathlon language, any male over 200 pounds is affectionately called a Clydesdale. I looked at him and saw that he was literally crying. Tears running down his face, sniffles, the whole works.

Not used to seeing this out of a grown man, I just stared at him until he half walked and half ran past me. I could not understand what circumstance could be so difficult that it could make a grown man cry like that. Was it physical, emotional, or both? Our paths were moving in parallel directions, with me on the spectators side of the cattle grates and him on the race course.

I asked him if he was okay. He shook his head no and looked at his feet. I wasn't quite sure what to say next as he slowly moved past me, so I lied and said in a deep Marine Corps voice, "You're looking strong. You got this." He just kept looking down, shaking his head and stumbling forward. Wow, I thought, this race must be tough.

That night, as we lay in bed in the hotel room staring at the ceiling and trying to grasp the enormity of the event we had just witnessed, my wife said that she was going to sign up for next year's race. She asked me if I would like to sign up as well. All I could say is that I would sleep on it.

Registration

The following morning, instead of driving home to Minneapolis like many of the other, more sane volunteers, we got up early and joined the long line standing on the Monona Terrace to register for the 2010 race. If you had volunteered for the race the day before, you got priority placement in the registration line the next day. Most years, the registration closed down after the previous year's volunteers had signed up and was not open for the general public to register.

The Monona Terrace is an enormous cement and glass convention center with a three-story parking garage attached to it. It is located in the center of Madison, a few blocks from the capitol, and is perched on the shore of Lake Monona. The building is ground zero for IRONMAN® faithful, as the race starts and finishes in and around its huge concrete walls. The two helixes that allow cars to roll in and out of the parking structure are the access points that athletes bike and run on. The architecture of the building reminds me of the Guggenheim Museum in New York.

By the time we got there the next day, most of the course was already broken down and cleaned up. Workers were packing trucks and sweeping streets. It looked like the circus train was pulling out of town. We chatted with the people around us standing in line to volunteer, and I felt a strange sense of fate about signing up for the race. I knew that I would have to take my fitness up several notches to be able to even get to the starting line. I also realized that I would need a lot of good luck to get to the finish.

People shared their five-minute stories of why they were lining up to register. Some people had been led to the line that day by journeys to overcome huge physical limitations such as cancer, limb loss, blindness, or obesity. Most had just worked their way up to this distance from the bottom. First 5Ks, then 10Ks, on to marathons, then short-distance triathlons, now the full monty. My overall sense from the people in line was that they were no more prepared or naturally gifted than Kathy and I were. In fact, everyone seemed pretty normal and generally likeable. This was important to me, as I tend to only like to be around people that I like to be around.

The line wound around the top floor of the parking garage of the Monona Terrace. Just twenty-four hours before, the same ramp had been packed with racers, gear, and excitement from the race. After an hour of slowly moving up in line, we got into the Monona Terrace building, and after weaving our way down a long hallway, we finally got to a registration table.

I stood in front of a volunteer seated behind a folding table. Against my better judgment, I signed up for the race and plopped down my non-refundable $550.00 registration fee. In my typical sarcastic way, I wrote that I was "drop dead sexy" on the part of the registration form where we were supposed to record chronic medical diseases or conditions.

The gravity of the event was on par with signing up for the Marine Corps, getting accepted into grad school, shooting my one and only trophy buck, having my first child, the 1996 Packers winning the super bowl and marrying my childhood sweetheart. The sense of something big, momentous, and life changing floated in the air and showed on the faces of the people who had just signed up.

It is said that a journey of a thousand miles starts with the first step, and now the first step was taken.

Better Judgment

One would think that, having completed ten marathons and four half-distance triathlons, a full-distance triathlon, such as an IRONMAN® race, would be well within my reach. Instead, this background gave me the solid understanding that I was completely out of my league in attempting this.

My previous tried and true marathon training program was an eight-week, half-assed training ramp up with a hard stop on alcohol and tobacco twenty-four hours before the race. Most often, I didn't stick to plan. Also, my current weight of 245 pounds was good enough to get me to an average marathon finish time of five hours and twenty minutes, but not slim enough to get me through the 140.6-mile race in less than seventeen hours. Lastly, my biggest fear, the four-hour wall I had experienced in every race before, was one that I knew would be toughest to overcome.

The "wall" is a term used by runners that signifies the point where you lose mental strength and physical power necessary to keep moving forward at your intended pace. Most often, athletes hit the wall because they either run out of calorie-based food fuel, hydration, or electrolytes. Many athletes hit this point at about mile twenty in a marathon. I generally hit it twice, once at about mile thirteen and then again at mile 22.

New York Marathon

While we hadn't really trained very hard in 2009, we did run the Anchorage marathon in July. I finished in five hours and thirty minutes. We were also registered for the New York Marathon in November.

Kath and I both had loose ties to Manhattan, and it was great to fly there and get caught up in the big city life. I was very nervous about finishing the marathon and kept asking myself how in the heck would I be able to run an IRONMAN® triathlon in under seventeen hours if I wasn't able to run a marathon in under five hours.

The race started out as good as can be expected. I was hoping to finish the course in four hours and thirty minutes, which was a pathetic finishing time for a guy my age. When the gun went off and we crossed the Verrazano Bridge, the excitement of the New York Marathon sunk in and I took off like a rocket. But taking off like a rocket is exactly what you don't want to do when you are running a 26.2-mile race.

Kath and I were separated in the mix of 40,000 runners at the start but somehow ran into each other at mile 5 and hung together until mile 16. At that point, my GI tract let loose and I started releasing fluids out of both ends of my body. This rapid release of fluids effectively drained my body of the necessary fuel and hydration I needed to finish running the race. My pace faltered from about ten minutes per mile down to probably thirteen minutes per mile.

I was dead, so I told Kath to go ahead without me to the finish. I still had more than ten miles to go and didn't want to slow her down. I went into a self preservation mode and began to alternate running for a few minutes with walking for a few minutes in a kind of survival shuffle. During the walking breaks, I alternated between vomiting and diarrhea. The nice thing about the design of the portable toilets on the race course that year was that there was a urinal right next to the toilet. This design allowed me to sit on the pot and puke in the urinal right next to me without standing up, conserving energy and time.

By mile twenty-two, I had totally hit the wall and could not run any more. I ended up walking the last four miles of the course, beat up but not beat down enough to quit. I limped across the finish line in a blisteringly slow time of 5:20. This put me in the top ninety-eight percent of guys my age who were running the race. The finishing time was awful, and I felt like death. Wow, I sucked as a runner!

The Saturday before the race, we had signed up to be part of the audience for *Late Show with David Letterman* on the Monday immediately after the race. We actually got invited to the taping along with a few hundred other marathon finishers. What a great show! Dave pandered to all of the marathoners with a top ten list about the race. He then interviewed the winner, Meb Keflezighi. I love New York!

Immediately upon returning from the New York Marathon, I caught the swine flu. Actually, I am pretty sure I had it during the run, as my throat was sore and I was measuring my time not by mile markers, but by distance to the next port-a-potty. For the next few weeks after the race, I felt like I had been ridden hard and hung up wet. Seven days after the race I actually went to bed for a full twenty-four-hour period. When I woke up, I noticed something interesting. I had lost over ten pounds, bringing me down to a manageable 230.

Now, I don't want you to think that I am obsessed with weight, but I am obsessed with data, and this is one thing that can easily be measured during race preparation. During the course of the next few months, my clothes began falling off my body as I slimmed down. Due to the huge amount of exercise, I was easily losing a few pounds a week. Within two months of starting to train, I went out and bought a new set of professional and casual clothes. Two months after that, I had to have the new clothes tailored to be even smaller.

Friends

As the training progressed, I began shedding friends as fast as I was losing weight. I place a lot of value in my friends, and I generally do something with at least one of them during lunch, after work, or on weekends. Instantly, IRONMAN® training drives a wedge between friends who will get you to the finish line and those who will not. As George W. Bush and many others have said, "You're either with us or against us." There is no middle ground.

For example, a friend who wants to go out for a beer and a smoke after work is one of the first who has to go. This person does not add to the miles that need to be racked up each week and slows you down with the incremental setback of one night of drinking and smoking.

Almost none of my friends were runners, and almost all of them were hardcore partiers. I stopped hanging out with these guys, and eventually we even stopped talking. That was then and this was now. A line was drawn. They needed to be culled from my portfolio. This forced segregation was extremely unfortunate, and while it was a survival technique, it was one of the worst collateral damages of the training.

Real Training Begins

In December my wife and I dove into the details of building a credible long-distance triathlon training schedule. We downloaded several stock plans from the Internet and bought a few books. Much of this information was overwhelming and, for the most part, extremely technical. I tried several times but just could not make sense of it. I could barely comprehend the technical details of V02 intake and didn't really care about lactic acid, much less utilize these metrics to guide our training.

Instead, we put together our own progressive training plan that would slowly build mileage and had periodic rest breaks, eventually leaving us ready for race day. Each day of the week was focused on a short swim, bike, or run and we would go progressively longer distances on the weekends. Our plan started us out at our current mileage and slowly built up to the full distance for each of the three events. We sprinkled our busy social, work, farm, and family commitments into this calendar. We also picked out a few key races and training camps to give us more formal experience along the way.

Several people have said that this self-directed, non-scientific plan was a big mistake. These same people have said that a more comprehensive, more intense, more professionally guided plan would have gotten us across the finish line in better shape with a faster time.

I would assert, though, that for people who are living a

well-rounded lifestyle, a calendar based on real-life knowledge of yourself and your commitments will keep you in the race. Conversely, a stock schedule put together around a gifted athlete with no social life, kids, or career could make you miserable.

A funny aside: I was changing clothes before work one morning in the locker room at the local health club. I was trading insults with a friend of mine who had just come back from a run. He is a very fit and gifted runner and was training to break a three-hour pace on his next marathon. I told him honestly that I was training for a six-hour marathon pace. He laughed and thought I was being sarcastic. Unfortunately, I was serious!

My First Visit to a Triathlon Store

I heard from a friend that there was a store in the Twin Cities that specialized in triathlon equipment and decided to drive up there one snowy January afternoon with my daughter. We walked into the store and were absolutely overwhelmed with the depth and breadth of gear available. There were shiny new carbon fiber bikes triple stacked on racks. Near them was a display of racing jerseys in a rainbow of colors and styles. Spandex shorts were pegged to the walls. The excitement of people who spoke the unique language of triathlon were everywhere in the store. It seemed like the only thing missing was glitter and unicorns. Of course, at this point I had run several triathlons, but I had never been to a place this specialized or just plain cool.

I had actually accomplished three half-distance triathlons at that point. I did the first one in 1986 on a mountain bike, wearing nothing but cut-off jeans, tennis shoes, and a smile. This included a 1.2-mile swim in 59° Lake Michigan without a wet suit. I was much more hardcore and much less into gear back then.

Before the latest half-distance triathlon, Kathy and I took our bikes out for only three short training rides. During the last training ride we tried to bike the full fifty-six miles and could only do it by stopping for Slurpees and Snickers bars along the way.

Back to the triathlon store, I walked up to a good-looking tri bike and started asking a clerk questions about it. The twenty something staff member lost patience with my rookie questions fairly quickly. After several condescending remarks, he looked at my daughter and asked, "Is this the bike you want or not?" I looked at the clerk sheepishly and said, "The bike is for me, not her." He rolled his eyes, and gave me an "oh." My daughter gave him the look that said "Yeah, my dorky dad is serious," and then we went on with the day.

With each subsequent trip to the shop I learned more about the triathlon and got closer to the people working the floor. Eventually the shop became my source of equipment and knowledge. And there was a lot to learn.

On my wife's first visit to this same triathlon shop, a technician asked what her level of competency was, and she said that she was a rookie. He gave her his credentials of Sprint- and Olympic-distance triathlons. He was obviously impressed with himself. He talked down to her a little while longer until I leaned in and told him that she had run thirteen full marathons and two IRONMAN® 70.3® races and was training for IRONMAN Wisconsin in eight months. This shaped up his attitude and eliminated his arrogant, better-than-you smack talk.

While these types of moments happened many times during the year and were somewhat comical, they always reinforced the audacity of our decision to sign up for an IRONMAN race. Now when I walk into a new triathlon store or training program, I let the F word (Finisher, as in IRONMAN Finisher) fly at the first chance—just so people know how bad I really am.

The Arrogant Athlete Psyche?

Another funny pattern among triathletes is the arrogance that often shows in their personalities. I have asked many fellow athletes if they have recognized this as well. I wondered if accomplished athletes just plain looked down their noses at too tall, too fat, over the hill, bald amateurs like me. The common thought is that because triathletes are generally cursed with antisocial attributes, they are often interpreted as arrogant.

While generalizing is dangerous, full-distance triathletes generally come from engineering or technical backgrounds. They also love to measure data about themselves. They would rather spend an afternoon training alone than spend it engaging in social activities. Also, they have an intense desire to compete and win. A friend of mine says that triathletes are the geeks of the sports world. I possess all of these attributes, so it is very easy for me to find these same faults in other people.

To be a successful triathelete, you need a genuine compulsive exercise behavior. A triathelete needs to train both morning and night for several days each week. It is unacceptable to hit the snooze on the alarm button and go back to sleep in the morning. To compete, you need to train. This level of effort needs to be deeply ingrained in the psyche of an athlete.

Spinning in January

As the year progressed, so did our training. Our health club offered three-hour spin classes every other Saturday. We followed these classes up with two-hour runs. I really gained speed and discipline from these sessions. This training helped us build strength, endurance, and confidence that would pay off months down the road.

Minnesota winters are cold. This makes outdoor bicycle training almost impossible for five months out of the year. Because of this, I pulled our two bikes up to the big screen TV in the family room and clipped them onto trainers. This allowed us to watch movies while spinning. I put my cell phone, home phone, channel changer, and computer next to the bike on a bar stool. This allowed me to do business while punching in the miles. What a great way to spend the cold winter evenings.

This home spinning in front of the TV began a Tuesday night ritual that we keep to this day. We begin by watching *The Biggest Loser* at 7:00 p.m. as we spin side by side. At 7:20, I hit the treadmill and run a mile. I jump back on my bike and resume spinning as Kathy jumps off her bike and begins running on the treadmill. We switch back and forth for the two-hour duration of the TV show.

We call this training routine a SPRIC. This stands for SPIN/RUN. This training time also turned into date night and helped to strengthen our relationship for the difficult times ahead.

Biking

A few years back, on a whim, I bought Kathy a nice Specialized triathlon bike for Christmas. It was low, sleek and fast. It looked like it was going a hundred miles per hour even while it was just standing still in the bike shop. I had never seen anything quite like it. With aerodynamic handle bars hanging over the front wheel and the bike seat a few inches ahead of the down tube for the pedals, it was a lean, mean, focused speed machine.

This forward slung configuration allows the athlete to cheat the wind by laying down instead of sitting upright. It requires less energy to keep the bike moving. It also puts less strain on the running muscles by using slightly different muscle groups than you would use in a traditional, more upright bike. The tradeoff for this forward slung position is a lot less sure-footedness on the road.

On a standard ten-speed road bike, you have plenty of stability and the flexibility to recover when you get into danger by, say, hitting a crack in the road. In fact, you can easily ride this style bike without your hands on the bars, balancing simply by moving your body. On a triathlon bike, you go from "Whoa, there's a bump in the road," to ass over tea kettle in a microsecond. Kath and I both wiped out several times that year. Our bodies slid along roads and suffered weekend war wounds. Thank God none of the accidents were too serious.

The feeling you get when you're clipped into a triathlon bike is nothing short of weightless free floating speed. The bike moves forward with minimal effort, and the nose-to-the-wheel riding position makes you feel like you are soaring. Sometimes when I am hard at it with a pack of other riders I feel like a jet pilot in formation with other flyers.

To control costs, I decided early on to not go out and buy a new carbon fiber triathlon bike like the one I got Kathy. Instead, I converted my Cannondale aluminum road bike into a racing machine by modifying it with aftermarket parts. This worked well enough, but since the 2010 race I have purchased a top-of-the-line carbon Felt triathlon bike with wind cheating Zipp wheels. It makes a huge difference over my old Cannondale in both ride, comfort and speed.

Several months into the training program, Kathy went out and upgraded from the Specialized to a brand new Quintanroo carbon fiber bike. This bike was specially built for women and fit her like a nice pair of blue jeans. I stuck with my aluminum Cannondale.

One tip that we got from Madison veterans was to switch out the rear cassettes on our bikes to lower gears. This new gearing would allow us to use less effort and spin up hills rather than power up them in a bigger ring. This change was relatively inexpensive and quick to make.

Veteran

When I got back to work after volunteering in Madison, a client's company newsletter announced that a clinical manager had just completed the IRONMAN® Wisconsin. He looked like an Olympic athlete on the cover of that newsletter, and I was actually somewhat intimidated by him. He was glad to take my call and I set up an informal lunch. Informal, that is, except for the list of thirty or so questions I had written down in my notebook to ask him. He was a wealth of information and said it was okay if I took notes.

He walked me through his training schedule, equipment, nutrition, race day plan, and gear. He was extremely positive and upbeat about the entire experience, and if he were selling entries to the race I am sure that almost everyone would want to buy one. I couldn't understand how someone who had gone through so much pain and abuse could be so positive. In fact, he said that he was going to take a recovery year and then do another one in 2011.

A couple of key things he said in this first meeting proved true:

1. Nutrition is the key to the race
2. Create a schedule you can live with and follow it closely
3. You are going to take a year off from family and friends
4. Train on the hills, as training in the flats will lead to failure

Almost none of these tips made sense to me at the time, but each one was understood and reinforced as we went through the year.

Coach

I also hired a professional coach. He did a great job, but I often thought that he was used to training professionals or committed athletes instead of slackers like me. Early on in May, I met him along with a group of thirty people and went for a mile-long open water swim.

He took one look at the way I fit into my wet suit and began using me as an example of how a wet suit should not fit. At 6'6" and 230 pounds, I am built like an eel. Wet suits are generally built for people who have an athletic wedge-shaped build. He showed the others how much space there was in my shoulders and how tight it fit in my midsection. I was a little embarrassed by this but sensed that what he was saying was generally right.

A hundred yards into that first open water swim, I started to hyperventilate. Every hundred yards after that I had to stop to doggy paddle and either get my runaway breathing under control, correct a horrible course deviation, or empty the water out of my goggles. It seemed like all of the pool training I had done during the winter had amounted to nothing. I finished dead last by several minutes. The look on my coach's face was like, "Seriously, dude? 140.6?"

I had several other interactions with him that went equally poorly. To this day, I am not sure if this was just his coaching technique or if he really could tell that I didn't belong on the course.

He deserves credit, though, for being part of the recipe that got me across the finish line. His advice on everything from gear, nutrition, and sleeping to swimming, running, and biking were critical. In fact, while I was pretty sure that I could outdrink, outsmoke and outshoot him, he could beat me at just about everything else.

I would highly recommend hiring a professional coach. I would also recommend that you interview several to find one who fits your personality before engaging in a contract.

Swimming

In 2006 I had the luxury of taking a few months off from work. I decided that I would spend each day in December hunting deer with a bow. At that time, my wife had picked up the habit of swimming laps in the local pool as a way cross train with the extreme running schedule that we were facing (we did four marathons that year). One day I decided to join her.

Like most other Wisconsin kids, I had grown up swimming in pools or outside in open water almost every day. In addition, my friends and I had a sense of adventure about long-distance swimming. We would frequently pick an island off on the horizon and dog paddle or frog kick out there with a dry bag full of beer and cigarettes. Now, in my mid-forties, I thought that I could just jump into a pool and lay out a mile-long swim.

I went to the pool each day for the next several weeks. The first few times, I could only swim a single length without stopping. Once on the other side, I would put a death grip on the edge for about thirty seconds to keep my heart from pounding out of my mouth and splashing into the pool.

I was so awful that during my first few times in the pool I would swim in a lane close to the edge because I feared drowning. That way there was something to grab onto to keep me from sinking to the bottom if I had to stop midway though a lap. Pools are generally shallow at one end and gradually become deeper as they go. Panic would set in each time I got near the deep end.

In the beginning, I crawled one length down and breast stroked one length back. By alternating my strokes, I kept from getting tired out too quickly and was able to increase my distance. My technique improved greatly with each trip to the pool, and pretty soon I was able to crawl ten, then twenty laps without stopping. Within a few months I swam my first mile.

Around this time I also watched a documentary on a guy who swam the English Channel. I set my sights pretty high after that and started visualizing the guy from the documentary when Kath and I went swimming. I brought this up to her and she laughed. I remember telling her that if a 28-mile English Channel swim was too far, we could probably work our way up to a 2.4-mile triathlon swim. She didn't think we could do that either.

Swimming is the great deal breaker in a triathlon. It is pretty easy to bike slowly when you are tired or even get off your bike and sit down for a rest. You can also walk or just plain lay down on the sidewalk and catch your breath if you are having problems running. The one thing you cannot do is stop swimming and put your foot on the bottom of the lake to take a breather. Most triathlons are done in water over eight feet deep. If you can't swim, you will not finish the race. It is that simple. In fact, every year, even though great precautions are taken to have lifeguards posted, several people across the country drown in the swim portion of the race. The year that we did the IRONMAN® 70.3® Racine race, two people drown in small races in Wisconsin alone.

Kath and I swam in open water whenever we got a chance. Generally, I would meet with a group of a dozen or so athletes before work at 6:00 a.m. and swim in a small lake near downtown Minneapolis. It was a half mile from one shore to the other.

Sometimes we would swim one mile, sometimes two. This training was critical to my ultimate success.

We also took a swim course called Total Immersion Swimming. This daylong course focuses you on working less and moving faster by improving your stroke. A series of drills and discussions are used to teach old dogs new tricks. The core message of the class is to lengthen your stroke and raise your shoulders by corkscrewing your body through the water. At the end, the swimmers' strokes are videotaped and critiqued by the class.

During the class I started playing around with breathing out on both sides of my stroke instead of just my right side. This allowed me to balance my body, keeping me in a straighter line. It also gave my muscles a more even workout, lessening muscle fatigue and cramping on a single side. Lastly, it gave me a better field of vision while I was swimming, allowing me to avoid course deviations and obstacles. This program was money and time well spent.

The Otter

Kath and I swam in any open water that we were near on the weekends. One memorable story was an open water swim we had at her parents' cabin in Antigo, Wisconsin. The cabin is on the windward side of a classic north woods muskie fishing lake. That day, the wind was whipping up the water and there were choppy waves with little white caps rising about two feet above the surface. It was a perfectly sunny day, complete with wispy clouds, singing birds, croaking frogs, and chirping grasshoppers. We put on our wet suits and walked down to the water's edge.

There was an island about a mile from the house. The plan was that I would swim out to it while Kathy and my youngest daughter Anna paddled in a canoe next to me. Kathy and I would then switch, and she would swim while I paddled back.

The way out was moderately difficult. It is very hard to strike a rhythm in choppy water. The current and the cross breeze kept blowing me off course. I remember drinking more water than was probably healthy as I turned my head into crashing waves to breathe. When I finally got to the island, I peeled off my wet suit and Kathy and I switched positions in the canoe.

On the way back, a family of otters swam up close and circled around our kayak. I was amazed by how big and happy their chubby little faces were. They effortlessly dove deep into the clear water and then came up and floated near us on their backs.

When they hit the gas, their bodies launched through the water. They stayed with us for about a quarter mile. It was very unusual to get this close to otters, and I could not help but be impressed by them.

I was very careful not to say anything about the otters to Kathy, as a swimmer in open water can get easily spooked by aquatic critters. In 2012, as I was writing this book, two women training for triathlons were attached by otters in Minnesota lakes.

April: The First Time on the Madison Bike Course

Spring came early to the Midwest in 2009, so in mid-April, Kath and I decided to tackle the Madison course by doing the forty-mile loop twice in a training ride. Nothing like getting right to it! We drove into Madison late on a Friday and spent the night at my sister Jayne's house. Jayne lives a few miles off the course, and her house was a good point to stage our gear and bodies for the night.

Jayne is a few years younger than me and has been a good friend, running partner, veteran marathoner, nurse, surrogate mother, and troublemaker throughout my life. She and her husband Mike were happy to see us and welcomed us into their house. The June Cleaver in Jayne had driven her to purchase water, fruits, and pasta to prepare us for the morning bike. We stayed up late into the evening talking about the race, kids, and life.

I wasn't thinking too much about hydration for the next day, and ended up splitting a case of beer with my brother-in-law. While drinking a dozen beers each seemed like a good idea at the time, the next morning was pure hell.

Actually, on the ride to the hotel, I talked Kathy, the designated driver, into routing us through the McDonald's drive-thru to get some early morning beef. While I recall the situation as being fairly tame, my sober driver recalls me talking large and laughing loudly about how we were going to crush the bike course in the morning. This doesn't surprise me, as I am a trash talker of the first order when drinking and oftentimes end up regretting doing the things my mouth talks me into.

Kath made sure I got out of bed early so as not to miss out on any of the fun we were planning to have that day. Actually, I thought she was doing this to punish me for drinking too much the night before. I was sweating hops and barley just getting the bikes ready in the morning sun. At the same time, I was trying to figure out how long it would take to complete eighty miles of the course. We usually biked about twenty miles per hour on flat courses, which would make this a four-hour ride. I could do four hours, I told myself.

The Madison course is a double loop with four major hills and many minor ones on each loop. It seems like you are either heading straight up or going straight down all day. One of the best things about the course in the summer is the number and caliber of riders who are training there. It is not unusual to see hundreds of fellow riders, and this really makes for a great experience.

On the up hills you go about ten or twelve miles per hour, and on the down hills you can exceed forty miles per hour. The course has a lot of turns and twists and at no point does the rider get bored with the scenery or terrain. The sun was merciless that day, baking the air to the mid-eighties. It was clearly the warmest day yet that year.

The heat, combined with the hills and hangover, made for a horrible experience. Kath and I ended up stopping about every fifteen miles—in Mt Horeb, Verona, and Cross Plains—each loop for a fifteen-minute break. During every break, I just laid in the grass on my back sucking wind and watching the clouds blow past. The heat was so intense that I felt like an egg frying in a pan.

People kept stopping and asking if I needed help or if anything was wrong. I couldn't really tell anyone I had a hangover. Generally speaking, long-distance triathletes don't drink, especially on the night before a big training ride.

When we neared completion of the second loop, I had a flat tire. I had to sit in the baking hot sun for another ten minutes and change the tube. When the tire was fixed, I swung my leg over the cross tube, clipped my feet onto the pedals, and finished the second loop. When Kath and I got into the car for the ride home, I felt completely nauseous and totally wiped out.

It took us almost eight hours—twice as long as we had planned—to complete the eighty miles. I crawled into the back seat of the car and immediately took a nap. After thirty minutes, Kath and I switched places. We drove the five hours back home switching back and forth as we tried to recover from the extreme day.

I thought that I would get stronger as the summer went on, but my results got progressively worse. I incorrectly attributed this to a combination of heat, hydration, and training. The pattern was always the same: start strong, then fall apart at four hours, finally struggle to the finish.

Nutrition—
The N Word

Every finisher needs to master his or her caloric intake, both on the course and off. If most people hit the wall at about four hours in a marathon because their body is out of fuel; imagine the consequences of conking out this early in a seventeen-hour race.

To begin getting your thoughts around the significance of nutrition for the long-distance athlete, think about the amount of food that it takes to get you through a normal business day. Now think about the amount that you would have to eat if your heart was pumping twice its normal resting rate for seventeen hours straight. I have pegged this down to 350 calories per hour for the entire race, or about 6000 calories total for the day.

I knew based on the New York Marathon that I had to improve significantly in this area, so I began experimenting with different nutrition products, such as gels and liquids. Each new product with its colorful and sexy package promised to be better than the previous one. Not one of them ended up working out. With each product, I got a quick lift that came in the front door and then I ended up crashing as I either vomited or splashed the liquid out of my back door.

My coach mentioned that Uncrustables (premade, prepackaged peanut butter sandwiches for kids) might be something I could try. They worked wonders! Time and again over the summer I noticed that my performance equaled my nutrition. Poor nutrition equaled poor performance. Good nutrition equaled good performance.

I also noticed that if I did not like the food that I was supposed to eat, I ended up not eating it. This compounded my problems by leaving me short on fuel. Therefore, healthy foods that also tasted good became part of my normal routine.

Further I learned that using complex carbs (such as whole wheat) as the main food group, gave me a stable base. Eating simple carbs (such as gummy bears) right before hills, gave me the necessary burst of speed needed to get up the hill. This balance of simple and complex carbs got me around the course in good shape.

I never paid much attention to my diet off the course, but I was able to remember a simple rule: browns are good and whites are bad. For instance brown bread contains whole wheats and complex carbs. White bread contains simple sugars. The same goes for brown rice, white rice, brown noodles, white noodles, and so on.

There are a lot of books, websites, and articles out there that discuss nutrition in great technical detail. The bottom line is this: you need calories to stay on the course. Some foods and gels that work well for some people do not work well for others. If you can eat it, and it stays in your stomach, it is good. If you cannot, it is bad. Those nuggets of wisdom will be the difference between success and failure.

Electrolytes

One day when we were training on our bikes, Kathy passed me and I really got angry with her for blowing by me. I assumed that she was passing me because she was stronger or in better shape than I was. I popped a couple of electrolyte pills right after she passed me and caught up to her shortly. Oddly enough, I also had a great attitude. It turned out that the anger and the fatigue I was feeling was a condition of the heat. By taking the electrolyte pills I could neutralize the effect and keep on going.

My wife and I called these electrolyte pills superman pills. I experimented with them on and off all summer and can assuredly tell you that these pills will improve your performance during a race in the heat.

Another funny story: I was watching the IRONMAN® 70.3® Racine one year and as usual it was scorching hot and horribly humid. At the halfway point of the run, an athlete's leg locked up and he tipped over and smacked headfirst onto the ground. He grabbed his cramped leg and rolled onto his back, spasming in pain.

I pushed my way through the crowd with several other people so we could get this guy off the road and into the grass. He was a total mess: red in the face, sweaty, and covered in snot. An EMT team just happened to be waiting nearby. They said that they were going to pull him from the course and put him on a stretcher.

He freaked at the thought of being pulled from the course and stood up as if he had been jolted by electric paddles. He popped a few electrolyte pills and started walking. We walked with him for about half a mile in disbelief and then just like that he said that he was okay and jogged off. I wasn't sure at the time if it was a testament to the raw determination of a competitor or the power of the electrolyte pills, but I now know firsthand that it was probably a little of both.

Decision Point

By mid-April, there were bigger things on my mind than an IRONMAN® triathlon. My wife and I were thinking of adding a young international child to our household and had begun the adoption process. When I say "we," I really mean that Kathy was leading the effort while I supportively tagged along.

We had raised two children of our own together already, and when they had moved out of the house to go to college it had left a huge hole in our lives. Not only were they gone, but so were their friends and their friends' parents, as well as the daily activity of getting them to and from school, sporting events, and jobs. All of the good and bad that surrounds having teenagers in the house was now forever gone. Kathy and I would come home at the end of the day and, for the first time since having kids, wonder what we were going to do that evening. Kathy was subconsciously looking to fill this hole by adopting a child.

To be honest, I was not very good with infant children. I didn't really appreciate diapers, bottles, child seats, late nights, early mornings, and having cereal and crackers mashed up in the back seat of my car.

I did very much enjoy having teenagers around, though, and I knew that we could provide a good home for a child to grow up in once he or she got past the infant stage, so I was supportive. However, I made it clear that this was not something that I would drive without her.

At the same time, I had landed a very lucrative contract with an out-of-state client. This contract would force me to travel every week, Monday through Friday, to their corporate headquarters in Cincinnati for the following year.

Making the decision even tougher, a local land owner had approached me through a third party and asked me if I would lease his land as part of my growing hunting preserve business.

Here I was facing four life changing decisions: competing in an IRONMAN® triathlon, adoption, out-of-state contract, and expanding our game preserve. Each of these activities would take much of my working hours and spare time for the next year.

As I dug into each opportunity and listed the pros and cons, it appeared that the options were mutually exclusive. In other words, I could only do one of the four things, but not all of them. In fact, the mental decision matrix was very complex.

If we were to proceed with the adoption, I could not take a full-time travel position, as it would essentially leave Kathy as a single mother.

If I was to proceed with the travel contract, I would have to drop out of the 2010 IRONMAN Wisconsin race, as I could not keep up the daily training and the extreme travel schedule at the same time. This also would leave Kathy essentially by herself five nights a week.

If I was to proceed with the hunting preserve, I would not be able to travel. Also, the time and money needed to establish the business would significantly impact my training and family time. Lastly, one of my misguided neighbors who was against the hunting preserve had hired a lawyer and begun a very public campaign of negativity and misinformation surrounding the business plans.

If I was to proceed with the triathlon, I would not have time to start my lifelong dream of the hunting preserve and could not travel.

All of this came to a head one morning. Each of the four options needed contracts signed on roughly the same day. For maybe the first time in my life, I made a decision that was not centered around my personal financial goals and decided not to travel and not to open the preserve, but to focus on growing our family with the adoption. This would also allow us to stick with the training plan and prepare for the race.

A few days after I made my decision, Kathy approached me and said that she didn't think the adoption was a good idea because it didn't make sense for me. So there it was. We were going to fill the hole in our life with IRONMAN® training schedule instead of an adoption or a new business venture. The decision was made.

One of the weird things about IRONMAN training is that it almost demands that your entire life be put on hold while you focus on training. This is nearly impossible for most people. Such a level of commitment really separates the athletes that move forward from those who self select out of the race. With the distractions of these life-changing decisions behind us, Kathy and I moved forward with IRONMAN training.

May Training

In May, our training began to hit decent volume and distance. Generally on Saturdays we would go between fifty and eighty miles on our bikes. On Sundays we would go for runs of five to fifteen miles. During the week we would go for shorter swims, bikes, and runs. With each week, we progressed in distance. We were wiped out at the end of each weekend and often napped on the drive back from whatever city we were training in as we took turns driving.

I began to get self-conscious about the number of times I was exercising per week and began lying to my friends about what I did over the weekend or the night before. It was just too hard to explain the amount and intensity of training that we were doing. At this point we were training about seven times per week. Several days each week, we worked out twice a day: once in the morning before work and once in the evening after.

It didn't seem like my level of fitness was progressing along with the distance, though. Each long ride ended with a long nap. My stomach would be a total mess, my heart rate would be at its peak, and my ego would be let down by my failure to hit interim training goals. I just didn't feel like I was ready to tackle IRONMAN® triathlon.

Truth be told, if Kathy would have said that she wanted to quit the training, I would have dropped out at any moment.

I did enjoy being in great shape; not many guys my age had the abs that I did. But I never once felt like the trade-off of losing time with friends and family was worth what ever minimal benefits we were getting.

Bike Shorts

Because we lived out in the country, it was difficult and dangerous to find a decent bike course to practice on. The two-lane country roads near our house were stone cold killers. Every year, joggers and cyclists were hit by cars on these roads. Because there were no shoulders on the roads, riding a triathlon bike with skinny tires was an especially dangerous proposition.

Because of this, we often drove up to 100 miles to reach one of Minnesota's many "rails to trails" pathways. These trails ranged in length from 25 to 100 miles. By mid-June, we were ready to do a full-on century ride, 100 miles, from Lanesborough to Harmony, Minnesota, and then turn around and drive back. As luck would have it, this trail was right in the middle of Amish country.

At that point in the summer, the relatively flat asphalt trail was still a stretch for us. We biked for about twenty miles at a time and then stopped to rest, eat, or water up. At the halfway point, we went into an old country restaurant in a classic small town. An Amish kid stared at my bike shorts, skin tight racing jersey, and funny-looking shoes. He leaned over and whispered to his friend, who snuck a peak at me and also laughed.

I didn't blame them. I didn't think that any of my boyhood heroes, such as John Wayne, Ted Nugent or Ronald Reagan, would ever wear bike shorts, so why the heck was I? I smiled back at the kids as I snacked on a piece of Amish apple pie.

Diabetes

In mid-June I was diagnosed with type-2 prediabetes during a routine lab test. My blood glucose level was abnormally high, so my doctor recommended a regime of diet and exercise to bring it under control. "Seriously?" I asked. "How could I possibly do a better job on either of those things?"

I was having problems keeping up with the training schedule as it was, and now this. I was worried that the diabetes would take me out of the race. At the same time, it may have been the excuse I was looking for to end the training and get on with a normal summer.

I started researching on the Internet and found that quite a few diabetic athletes had finished IRONMAN® races. They had rigged up insulin pumps to their bikes and found other ways to overcome their problems. Since I was only pre-diabetic, it didn't seem like this was the golden ticket excuse to keep me out of the race after all. Instead of knocking me out of the training, the diagnosis helped me focus more on removing sugar from my diet and fueling my body with more complex carbs.

Summer Training

By July, we had worked our way up to nine workouts, ranging from approximately fifteen to twenty hours per week. Our workout pattern looked like this:

- Monday - Weights
- Tuesday morning - Long swim (1-2 miles)
- Tuesday evening - Short bike (1 hour)
- Wednesday morning - Medium run (5-10 miles)
- Thursday morning - Short swim (.5-1 mile)
- Thursday evening - Short bike (1 hour)
- Friday - Short run (1-3 miles)
- Saturday - Long bike (50-100 miles) followed by a short run (1-2 miles)
- Sunday - Long run (13-15 miles)

Even though the training session increased in distance throughout the summer, I always felt the same at the end regardless of how far I had gone. Each session left me fatigued, nauseous, and feeling defeated. The only measurable result was more dirty laundry each day. I had expected to grow stronger as time progressed, but instead it seemed like I just kept barely making it to the finish.

WIBA

Given the fact that we were rookies, we were told by several veterans to sign up for an on-course coaching weekend. These weekend coaching retreats allow IRONMAN® wannabes to ride, run, and swim on actual segments of an IRONMAN race course. They also offer evening sessions that help teach the tools, tricks and tips necessary to finish the race. I didn't expect the retreat to make me faster, but rather just teach me how not to drown, crash, or twist an ankle.

These mini training camps also allowed Kathy and I to meet other athletes who were going through the same circumstances we were. After the camps were over, we ran into some of these new friends at different events throughout the summer. It seemed like many people had the same training schedules we had.

The first several coaching packages we looked at cost $500 to $700 dollars per person. In addition, we would have to pay for travel expenses. We couldn't commit to this cost, so we decided to look for a cheaper option. A friend told us about a free training course called the Wisconsin Brick Adventure (WIBA). WIBA is put on by good Samaritans for cheap people like us who are looking to experience the course. Realizing that you often get what you pay for, we decided to take a risk anyways and go to the session. If it didn't work out, we would spend more money on an expensive course later in the summer.

As usual, I got the pre-workout weekend anxiety as we packed up for WIBA. First we had to get home from work early and pack the car with all the necessary triathlon gear. Next, we had to get the dogs to the kennel, feed the livestock and poultry, pay bills, cut the grass, and perform basic house and car maintenance. Whatever didn't get done before we left probably wouldn't get done after we got back either. My blood pressure was high when we backed the car out of the garage and hit the road.

Actually, the packing process is an essential part of the triathlete's routine. If you forget to pack something, it is often difficult, if not impossible, to replace it on the course.

The five-hour drive was unremarkable. We got to Madison late in the evening, just in time for an athletes' dinner that also served as the first session in the WIBA training program. We parked our car downtown, near the Wisconsin capitol building, and walked along the street looking for the restaurant.

State Street was a blur of young kids looking for love, drinks, and good times. Homeless people sat on benches and asked for handouts. The smells of food, sweat, beer, and summer were in the breeze. We walked about halfway down the street and found the restaurant where WIBA was being held. We went inside and climbed upstairs to a conference room above the restaurant.

For one of the first times in my life, I didn't swagger into the crowd looking to talk smack and swap lies about an upcoming event. Kath and I sat down very humbly in the back of the room and tried not to make eye contact with any of the elite athletes surrounding us. I ordered a tall vodka tonic. Everyone else was drinking water.

During the meal, we exchanged small talk with people from all over the country. We soon found out that our chaotic lifestyle and lack of confidence in our abilities was pretty common. One of the people sitting across from me had actually run an IRONMAN® triathlon before. He told one heck of a horror story about the race.

He was a Clydesdale like me, possibly even heavier, and talked about the ordeal he had gone through at the IRONMAN Coeur d'Alene race the year before. He said that after he got off of the bike, he was in such bad shape that all he could do was walk the marathon. I asked him how long it took him to walk such a distance. He said that it had taken him almost seven hours. I asked if this got him to the finish line within the cut-off time of seventeen hours and he said yes. I made a mental note to make this my fall-back strategy.

We listened to the WIBA program, which included a pro athlete talking about the course. The pro gave a lot of tips on what to do and what not to, and we soaked up his information. He gave us small hints on how to tackle the extreme course. For example, he advised that we shove ice down the front of our shorts to keep cool during the running portion or the race. He also suggested putting a can of Coke in your special needs bag to give you something to look forward to on the run. He was an endless source of knowledge.

We slipped out of the room shortly after the seminar was over and walked back out onto State Street. The evening traffic had picked up, and there were kids walking in every direction. We walked quietly back to the hotel room at a slow pace to conserve energy for the next day.

Saturday morning, we woke up early and went down to the shores of Lake Monona. Everyone brought their wet suits and we swam in the lake for the first time. The unusual size and pattern of the waves in this lake worried me a little, but it was overall a great preparation for swims to follow. At this point I didn't have a whole lot of open water racing experience, so I was quickly educated on the differences between racing in a pool and racing in a lake.

One of the biggest differences is that while it is pretty easy to swim a straight line between the lane markers in a pool, there are no straight lines on the bottom of the lake. Because of this, it was very easy to take a ninety-degree turn and swim ten or twenty yards off course before figuring out that you were heading in the wrong direction.

The fear of drowning that was constantly in the back of my mind came to the forefront anytime I wasn't thinking about getting tangled in the weeds, attacked by a carp, hooked by a fisherman, or run over by a boat. Such anxiety can raise a swimmer's heart rate to the point that it can cause hyperventilation.

Like everything else in a triathlon, these anxious fears were overcome by putting mind over matter. If you don't mind something, then it likely didn't matter. Eventually, I made it to the end of the mile-long swim course, even though I was a little worn out and embarrassed by my pathetic performance.

Later that morning, we transitioned from swimming to cycling. The bike course was an even bigger disaster than the swim, as I fell apart midway through the second loop of the course. When I say fell apart, I mean I hit the wall so hard that I couldn't pedal my bike faster than a few miles per hour without becoming too dizzy to stay upright. Because of this, Kath and I cut the second loop short and took a straight but hilly road back toward where we had parked. After pushing for a few miles, it became clear that I couldn't even make it back to the car.

The sun was so hot that it felt as though there were three

of them out that day, each focused on burning me up. I was cramped up, and I had to get off my bike and walk it up one of the bigger hills. I finally had to lay my bike down under a tall shade tree on the side of the road and take a breather. This pattern of working my ass off and falling short began to wear on me. I sat under the tree soaking wet with sweat and wondering what the fuck I was doing attempting this race.

I didn't look good in spandex and hated how much free time I had spent training. I also really didn't like talking to people who would rather have a sports drink and a granola bar than a cold beer, a cigarette, and a grilled steak.

As I was lying on the ground on the side of the road in the shade of the only oak tree for a mile in either direction, a local guy pulled up in his car and asked me if I wanted a ride back to town. The last thing I was worried about was taking a ride from a stranger. I said hell yes and piled my bike and Kathy's into his car. He drove us back to the course's starting point, where the faster athletes were already finishing. Beaten and disgusted with my performance, we packed up our bikes and got the hell out of Madison.

On the drive out of town, I looked over at a homeless man begging for change. We made eye contact and I rolled down my window to give him a dollar. As I dug in my pocket, I suddenly felt it like it would be better for both of us if I just gave him my bike. He would get a solid means of transportation and I would be done with the silly IRONMAN® training. It was clearly a win/win situation.

Kathy thought I was joking at first but quickly realized that I was serious. Our car was stopped in the middle of a busy street, oblivious to the traffic behind us, as we argued about my next steps. Once again, she talked me off the ledge by saying that I should donate my bike to a homeless guy AFTER the race, not before it. Slightly defeated, I rolled up the window and drove off, leaving the guy wondering what had just happened.

Once again, my stomach was a mess from the weekend's training. We drove the five hours back to Minneapolis alternating sleeping and driving cycles and avoiding discussion of the weekend's debacle. This was the first time I really considered dropping out of the IRONMAN® Wisconsin race. I decided to go to the IRONMAN® 70.3® Racine race the next weekend and judge my future prospects based on performance there.

IRONMAN® 70.3® Racine

As was now our typical process, we packed up the car and left Friday night for the seven-hour drive to Racine, Wisconsin. It was a beautiful evening, and driving through the Wisconsin country-side as we anticipated the Sunday race was a pleasant experience. We had the radio cranked up, our sunglasses on, and our racing bikes racked on the back of the Beamer. When we got closer to Racine, we started seeing other cars with "IRONMAN" window stickers and expensive bikes on their racks. Several thousand IRONMAN faithful were descending on the town.

We had run the IRONMAN 70.3 Racine race two times before. We had improved a little each year, and I was really look-ing forward to shaking the ghost of the previous week's failure at the WIBA training camp. This year, I was targeting a ten-minute improvement over the previous year. Hell, given all of the train-ing we were doing, I felt sure that I would be throwing down a thirty-minute improvement or more.

In my first Racine race, I finished third from last. The sec-ond year, I knocked almost an hour off that time. This time my goal was to finish in six-and-a-half. It was a relatively simple goal for an average athlete, and it would put me in the middle of the finishing pack.

My confidence level was high as we checked into the motel. We had trained much greater distances than we were going to race that day. In addition to confidence, I also had a few tricks and a bag full of treats to get me through the day.

My new biking tricks included a strategy of starting out slow and not exerting myself too much on uphill climbs. The treats included sugar-free energy drinks and bars that could deliver 350 calories per hour during the expected six-and-a-half hours I was going to be on the course.

The swim course had changed this year and was now an elongated U-shape. Even with all of my open water swimming experience and the safety measures that are in place, I still got pre-race panic thinking about all that could go wrong. As I stood knee-deep in the water with 2,000 other athletes waiting for the start, even the pee filling my wet suit didn't warm me up in the 62° F Lake Michigan water.

The starter's gun went off shortly after "The Star Spangled Banner" played, and the pros were off in the first wave. Kath went off in the fifth wave with the other 45- to 50-year-old females, and I went off in the seventh wave with the other over-the-hill males. A guy I had been chatting with before the race mentioned to me that there were so many young people doing this race that he felt like a teacher walking around at preschool.

Swimming straight out into oncoming waves with athletes competing for space around you is a recipe for hyperventilation, and boy did it hit me. As I rounded the first corner, I had to stop and let athletes pass me as I ripped my goggles off and gasped for air. A hyperventilation attack at that point in the course was especially untimely. Anytime I opened my mouth to take a breath, it was filled either with a wave of icy Lake Michigan water or the fist or foot of another swimmer.

Okay, so stopping and treading water was a bad idea. I briefly thought about swimming back to shore and quitting the race right there but decided that it was not much farther to swim to the finish than it would be to swim back to the start, so I laid down in the water and started swimming.

By this point in my training, I was easily knocking down two-mile swims in the pool. I was also swimming a mile at a time in a small lake near work. What I wasn't used to was swimming in large, open bodies of water with huge groups of people surrounding me and very little to sight on. My course was like that of a drunken sailor on a Friday night, swerving back and forth from left to right.

Overall, it is safe to say that the swim did not go very well. Because of the huge problems staying on course, I expended more energy then I should have. Also, the anxiety of being in the cold water among a large group of swimmers kicking and splashing each other left me dizzy and disoriented. I finished the 1.2-mile swim 15 minutes slower than I had expected to. When the shore finally reached up and touched my feet, I thanked God and ran barefoot up the sand to transition to the bike.

The transition went slower than it had the year before. Also, I can never quite figure out how to change clothes quickly, so I lose my mind and forget things. As I was running with my bike outside of the transition area, I realized that I had forgotten to put my electrolyte pills in my jersey pocket. I didn't think this would be a problem at the time, but this was one of many mistakes I would make that day.

The bike course went well from a time perspective, as I hit my three-hour goal, but it was not a very enjoyable experience.

The course had a lot of cracks and bumps in the road, making the ride a teeth-chattering, neck-breaking experience. The sun came out early, making me sweat like a used car salesman at church. I started getting dizzy and instantly regretted leaving the electrolyte pills behind. With that said, I did hit my time goal of three hours on the 56 mile bike course.

The transition from the bike to the run was even worse. It started raining buckets just a few minutes before I pulled into the transition area. Rivers of rainwater rolled through the parking lot and started washing everyone's gear away. In the deluge, I put on my bike jersey backward and had to peel it off my wet body to put it on the right way. Unbelievably, I accidentally left my electrolyte pills in the transition area once again as I headed out on the run.

To be honest, it was more of a walk than a run. Running after you get done swimming one mile and biking fifty-six is hard, painful, and just plain no fun.

Kathy developed a strategy of picking equally spaced items, such as light posts, mailboxes, or street corners, and using them to mark off periods of running and walking. This strategy gives you short term goals and keeps you moving until you are ready to give it your all.

I started out walking for three light posts and then running one. I then ran two and walked two. Eventually, I ran three and walked one then ran four and walked one. I kept asking myself during this humbling experience why I was going to attempt the full-distance triathlon in Madison when I couldn't even finish the half-distance with a dignified run time. At mile three, I resolved that I would finish the Racine race and then tell my wife that I was quitting IRONMAN® training. I would get back to normal life the following weekend by going boating.

My parents were planning to attend the Racine race, but I had neglected to touch base with them ahead of time to arrange a meeting place. I looked for them at the places they had been stationed in the two previous years, but they were not there. While I didn't see my folks, I thought about them to keep my mind off of the run.

I was completely spent by mile five. The heat had won. It melted me down into a fraction of the runner that I normally was. I kept pushing on, running a few light posts and then walking a few. It was painful, but eventually I approached the end. As I came down the hill that signaled the end of the race, I looked one more time for my parents in the crowd but did not see them. I finished the race and was greeted by my wife (yes, she finished before me). Finally, as we were walking out of the finisher's chute, I saw my mom and dad.

It was smoking hot out, maybe 95° F and humid. The kind of heat where everything moves in slow motion. The kind of heat that makes it hard to breathe. The kind of heat that makes your clothes wet with sweat if you walk across the street from one air-conditioned building to another. I looked like death, and I was covered in salt.

I was very happy to see my parents. We talked about the race and traded family gossip. My parents were dripping with sweat just standing and talking to us. The sun was merciless. My mom asked me several times why I was going to do a race twice as long as the one that I just finished. I told her that I wasn't going to do it after all. That I decided there, that day, that I was going to drop out of IRONMAN® Wisconsin and get my life back to normal. This seemed to make her as happy as it made me.

My parents asked us if we wanted to meet them for lunch, but we told them that we didn't have time because we had to get on with the seven-hour drive back to Minnesota. I felt bad about not being able to get together with them, but this was endemic of IRONMAN® training. You never have time to just sit and talk to people who are important to you. I didn't know it at that moment, but this would be the last time I ever saw my mother.

On the drive back home, I told my wife of my decision to quit the IRONMAN Wisconsin race. She suggested that I do the training program for one more week before making a final choice, and I reluctantly agreed.

Once home, my wife and I hung our finisher's medals from our ego mirror, a family ritual that we had performed many times over the previous several years.

The Ego Mirror

In a prominent place in our kitchen, we have a mirror with a rich hand-carved wood frame. We keep our finisher's medals here. Hers are draped over the left side, and mine hang on the right. The number of medals has grown over the years. By 2010, we had each completed roughly a dozen marathons, twice as many half-marathons, and several half-distance triathlons. Each of these races had given us medals as we crossed the line.

Each medal is an individual work of art. The typical medal has a colorful ribbon that hangs around the athlete's neck and a Texas-belt-buckle-sized gold or silver medallion. Oftentimes the medallion is shaped and engraved to memorialize the event. My first Twin Cities Marathon medal was shaped like an oak leaf to recognize the fallen autumn leaves along the course. My Marine Corps Marathon finisher's medal has a depiction of the famous Iwo Jima flag raising cut into its face. The Walt Disney World® Marathon awards Mickey Mouse medals to marathon finishers, Donald Duck medals for finishing the half-marathon, and Goofy medals for finishing both races in the same weekend. All of the medals hanging together on the mirror make for quite a shrine of runner's bling.

In many of the tougher races, I hung in to the finish just to get the medal. To the best of my knowledge, the medals have no monetary value, and if you look them up on the Internet, you will find that they are just about the only thing you can't find for sale on Craigslist.

In 2010, I was involved with a charity called Medals for Meddle. Finishers donated their medals to the charity, which then awarded them to children who were facing terminal diseases as recognition for their arduous effort. As we hung a medal over a child's neck, we said, "The athlete who worked so hard to finish the marathon and get this medal thought that he would donate it to you in recognition for all that you have gone through over the last year." The kids' families often teared up during the delivery, and so did I.

As powerful as it was to give a child a medal, I could never quite part with any of mine. I guess that says a lot about the value of a finisher's medal, and a lot about myself.

Each morning, as I get ready for work, I look into the ego mirror and see the medals from all of the races that we have finished. The depth and breadth of the pile is expansive, covering many states and events. Somehow this gives me a little extra strength to get through the toughest days. Yes, it's cheesy, but it is part of the experience that makes us, and keeps us, endurance athletes.

Mom's Death

On August 12th, 2010, my mom died of a heart attack in her sleep. I was at work in Minneapolis when my sister called me, and I couldn't believe what she was telling me. I had just seen my mom several weeks before in Racine and there hadn't been any warning signs. I immediately called my wife and two daughters, who were both out of state at college. We hastily put together a plan to meet in Minneapolis and then drive to the funeral in Wisconsin as a family rather than come in at different times.

One more time that summer, I packed up the BMW for a drive to Wisconsin. This time it wasn't for training but to go to my mom's funeral. My mom had really hated the triathlon life style. She didn't like the fact that it prevented us from spending time with her. She also saw what we looked like at the end of a race and couldn't correlate the pain with any type of gain. On a recent visit to my parents' house, my sister had told me to hide the bikes on the back of our car because it would make mom mad if she saw them.

Unfortunately, we had a non-negotiable training schedule to keep. Taking a whole week off for my mom's funeral just wasn't in the cards. I thought maybe we could slip out of the funeral process for a few hours each day and keep up the training. The program was so intense that I was seriously wrestling with finding a way to pack in training hours while at my mom's funeral. How pathetic! I reluctantly packed our bikes, wet suits, and running shoes along with our funeral clothes and got the family into the car for the six-hour drive home to Wisconsin.

The next week was not as hard on me as I would have thought it would be. It hadn't really sunken in yet that my mom was gone. I went out each morning and ran or biked to feed the training disease. This time away from the funeral proceedings was cathartic and helped me get my head around the enormity of the loss. On one particularly long run, I cried for about an hour, picking up the pace and letting my emotions drive me to a sustained full-on sprint. It had been so long since I had cried that I could not even remember the last time.

At my parents' house, I saw a lot of people I hadn't seen in years. They asked me what I was doing and how my wife and kids were. It seemed like my old friends had aged much more than my wife and I had. Most had huge Wisconsin beer bellies and were showing the signs of being in their late forties. It seemed like Kath and I hadn't really changed a whole lot, as the intense training had kept us at roughly the same weight we had been in high school.

A few of my high school friends tried to one-up me with stories of their recent athletic or business prowess. For one of the few times in my life, I checked my ego and let them talk about the 5K races and softball seasons they were participating in. I was four weeks away from 2010 IRONMAN® Wisconsin race and didn't feel like explaining the magnitude of the event or the insanity of the weekly training.

I volunteered to give the eulogy at the funeral and based it on seeing my mom at the finish of the race of life. My mom was not an athlete, an entrepreneur, or an academic, but she brought these qualities out in everyone she surrounded herself with. Between my brother, sisters, and in-laws, we had run almost fifty marathons, and many of us owned and operated our own companies. Our nephews and nieces were even more successful.

While we grew up in the lower middle class (I was actually the first male in our family to graduate from college) my mom really developed a strong family of overachievers and we had jumped up to a life of seemly unlimited resources, social connections and financial privilege. The church was packed for the funeral, and she will be missed by many. She had a strong faith in God and lived a saint's life. We drove back home to Minneapolis in silence. I think about my mom every day. We really miss her.

Breakdown

As an ex-Marine, I know how to throw a fit. I have had a flash temper my whole life and it never hides very far from the surface. When my temper comes out, I can lay the smack down in a cadence and volume that scares even me. It burns deep within me and takes me places that I know I should not be. Sometimes I punch, break and throw things, turning the situation even worse and making it harder to come back from the edge.

I am not sure what a nervous breakdown is, but I can tell you what happens when you train for something for many months and repeatedly fail to hit your milestones. Your frustration catches up with you and you break down—old school. It happened to me one day after work as I was using a chainsaw to cut down trees on the farm.

I started muttering to myself, listing the things I didn't like about the training regime. The saw's engine was snarling loudly as the chain ripped through tree trunks, covering the fact that I was talking out loud.

- I don't like wearing spandex bike shorts.
- I don't like sweating my ass off all the time.
- I don't like the anxiety that I got when it came time to swim.
- I hate packing all the necessary gear.
- I keep looking for the thrill of victory, but I only find the agony of defeat.

I was working myself into a frenzy, and as the chain saw was whining, I began screaming. I HATE ALL THE MONEY THAT WE'RE SPENDING ON TRAVEL, GEAR, KENNELS, SPE-CIAL FOODS, AND LODGING. The more I verbalized the higher the anger level climbed.

I started throwing things, and then the monster came out. I was really screaming—loudly. I hate bikes, I hate running, I hate not having friends, I hate not having time, I hate not sleeping, I hate the smell of sweat, I hate checking the weather forecast on my cell phone all the time. Finally, it sank in. Completing an IRON-MAN® triathlon was a meaningless goal. The people who accomplished it were not like me, and it took too much time and effort. Fuck it. I was done for sure.

Once again, I had decided to quit the race. Or so I thought. I packed away the chainsaw and drove home, where Kath was waiting for me to pack the car to go to Madison for the second training camp.

. . . . So I did . . . .

The more triathlon crap I threw in the car, though, the madder I got. Once we had gotten in the car and begun driving, I told Kathy I was out of the game. She patiently listened but never acknowledged any of the issues I raised. Three hours into the drive, she quietly said, "Why don't you just make it through this weekend and make up your mind after it's over?" Tired out from the emotional explosion I had just gone through, I agreed, and we drove the last two hours to Madison in relative silence.

Quitter

I have only quit three things in my life.

I quit smoking in 1985 after getting out of the Marine Corps. Not being very good at quitting, I still smoke when I drink and even sometimes when I don't.

I quit little league baseball because I couldn't hit a ball off of a batting tee. To this day I have no trouble hitting a moving ball but will just plain miss any ball that is standing still.

I quit the Ridge to Bridge marathon after running the first thirteen miles. I had some problems with my knee and decided at the halfway point not to keep going. I walked around with this disappointment for many months afterward.

Those who say that it is nobler to attempt something and fail than it is to not attempt that thing at all have probably never failed at anything of importance.

Back to Madison for the Second Training Camp

The second training camp was a replay of the WIBA training camp in every way, other than that it cost a lot more money. After we checked into the hotel in Madison, we went out for a brief swim in Lake Monona. As before, the pattern of the waves, the lay of the shore line, and my inability to properly sight a fixed course resulted in me finishing dead last out of the other swimmers. I further embarrassed myself by accidentally kicking the girl who finished second to last in the face as our paths crossed.

Adding insult to injury, the coach singled out my lack of skills to the other swimmers a couple of times. What an ass that coach was. Here was a guy I could outfight, outhunt, outdrink, and outsmoke, and he was making jokes about my ability to swim in a straight line. I probably made more money in a few hours than he made in a week I didn't need this joker's crap.

After the swim training session was over, I cooled off, then Kath and I went out to dinner with the group so we could meet the other athletes. One of the coaches that weekend was a professional triathlete. He had finished third in the IRONMAN® 70.3® Racine race a month before and was as modest about that as you could possibly be. He told a few funny stories at dinner. One of the stories began when a girl asked him how many times he had gotten off the bike to pee during the IRONMAN® 70.3® Racine race.

He told her that he never got off the bike and just peed in his shorts as he rolled down the course. The girl was shocked, and everyone else at the table smiled.

I couldn't believe that the common knowledge that peeing in your pants was expected had never been shared with me. What else didn't I know?

Many of the other athletes also had funny stories. The biggest benefit of going to a camp like this is meeting other people who are going through similar circumstances as you are.

One of the more memorable people I met was a lawyer from Minneapolis. He was a very strong biker who liked to drink tequila and needle people into saying things they shouldn't. He brought up an interesting discussion about hitting the wall at the race in Racine after he got off the bike.

The consensus about hitting the wall that night was that it was tied to the athlete's body running out of fuel. The trick is to eat foods that you can keep in your stomach while moving around. Greasy foods don't tend to stick around long, dry foods don't go down easy, and wet foods are hard to carry and handle. The packaging of the nutrition is also important. It is difficult to unwrap a hamburger and fries while cycling twenty miles per hour in a pack of athletes.

My greatest nutrition barrier is that I have a relatively weak stomach and can only tolerate certain foods during the extreme bouncing that occurs in a marathon or an seven-hour bike ride. Because of this, traditional sports gels and drinks only made my stomach explosive.

The discussion that night made me reevaluate my food plan for the weekend. I reworked my plan to include a lot of easy-to-chew carbs and would find out shortly if my mix of peanut butter sandwiches and whole grain foods would get me to the finish.

Another athlete at dinner that night happened to be a co-worker of mine. When he hit his mid-life crisis point, he had not purchased a Corvette. Instead, he bought a Corvello, a high-end racing bike. I got to know him during the 112-mile training ride the next day, and after I quit the ride early, he ended up finishing the course with my wife.

Yes, I quit the ride early. My spirits were in the tank after yet another attempt and failure just to make it around the bike course without swimming first or running after. This time I dropped out of the bike course sooner than I had at WIBA. It was the dog days of August and the temperature on the bike course was in the mid-nineties. The black asphalt road was bubbling tar from the heat of the midday sun. The air was heavy and each breath scorched my lungs. It felt like we were in a blast furnace. It was hard to even walk outside of an air-conditioned space, much less race a bike on a hilly course that day.

My true friends were out on their boats drinking beer, having fun, and staying cool. They were drunk texting me every few hours with "when are you going to get here?" text messages. I was stuffed into spandex shorts, sweating my tail off, wasting another summer weekend training, and quite frankly, hating life.

Sixty miles into the course, the bottom of my endurance tank dropped out. No matter how deep I drew, there was no energy left. My muscles were cramping, my head was swirling, and my mind was not in the game. Mirages of heat waves rose from the road as I looked for an oasis.

Making matters worse, the chain jumped off my bike whenever I cranked hard on the pedals. Every time the chain derailed, I had to stop the bike and get off. Then I had to remove the water bottles so that they wouldn't spill and lay the bike on its on its side. Then I had to pry the chain out from between the sprocket and the frame. Oftentimes, my hands would slip from the chain, cutting my knuckles on the points of the sprocket. Once the chain was free, I had to finagle it back in place on the derailer and gears and spin the pedals a few times to ensure that it would stay in place. Once the chain was fixed, I then reversed the process and put my water bottles back in their racks and stood the bike back up. The whole exercise took around ten minutes.

During this process, my hands would get covered in bike grease, and each time I wiped the dripping sweat from my brow I smeared grease on my face. The skin on my knuckles was torn from contact with the sharp sprocket points, and blood dripped slowly onto my jersey and equipment.

Every stop I made to fix my bike distanced me further from the pack of riders. Frustration set in from not being able to keep a steady pace. Later that year, I would find out that the cause of this problem was a stretched chain. But even if I had known then that this was the issue, there weren't any spare chains available nearby.

On a brief but intensely steep uphill on the way to Mt Horab, the chain jumped off the ring once again. My forward momentum came to a halt as the chain jammed between the sprocket and the frame. I quickly started to roll back down the hill. My feet were clipped into the peddles, limiting my ability to stop my backward slide. An instant later, pow! I tipped over and smacked the concrete, skinning my knee and bruising my shoulder. My physical pain was minor, but the impact to my confidence was huge.

As I lay on the scorching roadside staring at the sky, I suspected that this was God's way of telling me once again that I was not cut out for this course. I had given it my best shot not just once but many times that year and could not make it around. This was the last straw, and I again decided that I was officially done with IRONMAN® racing.

There was a support van following our group around the course. The driver saw me laying on the ground like a road killed raccoon and popped out of the van to ask if I was okay or if he could help fix my bike.

I said no.

For maybe the sixth time that day, I laid the bike on its side and pried the chain from between the frame and the sprocket. Once again, I skinned my knuckles, and my hands were a bloody, greasy mess. After I put the chain back on, I flipped the bike onto its wheels and did a quick damage check.

Like the skin on my knuckles and knees, the tape on the handle bars was scraped from hitting the asphalt. Other than that, there was no other damage. With a cool head and calm demeanor, I turned my bike around and began to head home to the hotel.

The sag wagon driver pleasantly asked me where I was going and offered to put the bike in the van and drive me. I knew that the bike ride back would be long and hilly but decided that I would leave the course under my own power, on my own terms, and with dignity, not defeated in a support van.

On the way back to the hotel, I came to a heavily populated stoplight in the middle of Madison. I forgot to unclip my shoe from the bike pedal and fell over for a second time that day. Even though I was stopped, I somehow slid across the ground and got more road rash as I did a three point landing on my elbows, knees, and face.

Man, was I in bad shape. As I stood up, it felt like the whole world was stopped and watching this over-the-hill klutz in spandex shorts make an ass of himself. I walked my bike across the intersection and sat down in a parking lot to assess my latest wounds. The sun was blazing on my skin. I squirted some water on the scrape on my knee, picked a few pebbles out of the bloody mess on my elbow, and then drank the rest of the bottle.

My neck was aching from hunching over the handle bars all day. My butt was sore from sitting on the mostly unpadded seat. My thighs were tense and shaky from powering up the hills. I just wanted to go to the hotel and get in bed.

I figured that I was about five miles to the hotel and that it would be quicker to ride then walk home. I climbed back onto my Cannondale and slowly pedaled home. In total, I ended up biking twenty-four miles back to the hotel from where I had quit the course, stopping twice to nap. This put my entire mileage for the day at just under eighty miles—not too far off the intended 112.

Back at the hotel, I shed my biking gear and jumped in the shower to cool down and clean up. The warm water felt great against my skin. The salt from the dried sweat that covered my body stung a little as it washed into the cuts and scrapes that I had collected that day. I started thinking about all the things I was going to do now that I had officially quit training for the race.

For sure I was going to get back into boating. Minnesota summer was so short and I missed my friends and the water. I was going to blow the dust off my golf clubs and get my game back on. I was going to fix the fences, clean the water troughs, build new gates, and get my livestock back under control at the farm. I was going to make up for lost time with family and friends and enjoy the summer! A huge calm came over me. I went to a happy place in my mind.

I packed up the hotel room and walked all the gear down to the car. I was in such a good mood that I chatted with people as I walked down the halls and probably even whistled a happy tune. After the car was packed, I grabbed a beer and sat down in a plush leather chair in the air-conditioned lobby. The only thing to remind me of the horrible day that I had just had were the bumps, bruises, and scrapes covering my body.

The lead riders were already coming through the front door of the hotel. They were spent from riding in the 90° F heat. The athletes were congratulating each other on finishing the brutal ride and telling war stories about different parts of the day. A few of them quickly put on tennis shoes and then went out for a run to simulate the transition on race day from bike to run.

One of the guys recognized me and saw me relaxed and cleaned up in a cotton T-shirt and bermuda shorts. He walked over to me and sat down. He asked how my day went and said that he had lost track of me around mile fifty. I told him that I had packed up and got going off the course when the going got tough at mile sixty. I mentioned that I had quit the entire training program and that as soon as my wife got back and our bikes got loaded, I was getting the hell out of Madison—for good.

He winced as I told my story and then kind of jumped back, as if my quitter's attitude was contagious and he didn't want to catch my bad juju. I also noticed that the way that he looked at me had instantly changed. Our conversation had gone from a peer to peer discussion to one where one athlete was talking to a lesser human. Well, if I was now on the outside of the triathlete circle, it sure felt like a good place to be! I ordered another beer while I waited for Kathy to come in.

When she got into the lobby, I loaded our bikes as she went out for a short run. She looked like hell but had gone the distance and completed the course in the heat. On the ride home we were upbeat for different reasons. Kathy was excited that she was ready for the race and I was glad to finally be done with this stupid experience and damn happy about it.

Possum

When we pulled into the driveway, I looked over and saw a possum hanging by his tail from a tree in the wooded ravine. He looked so happy with his ruffled white hair and tiny red paws. He had been hanging around (no pun intended) all summer and it was kind of comforting to see him waiting for us to get home.

The possum had always been a lucky symbol for me. I had invented something I called the possum strategy for running marathons years before. With the possum strategy, I would start the race slow and just lope along for the frst thirteen miles conserving energy. After hitting the halfway point, when it looked like I would finish in horrible time, I would turn on the heat and finish the last thirteen miles strong.

The possum strategy was the reverse of the cheetah strategy, which I had used for years before that. In the cheetah strategy, I would start fast and then run faster. The cheetah was a miserable disaster any time I ran more than fifteen miles, as I would crash and burn and then end up in a slow run walk, barely crossing the finish line.

Once in the house I took two sleeping pills with a vodka martini and went to bed. As I lay, I couldn't help thinking about the possum hanging from the tree.

The Road to Kona— The Breakthrough Moment

The very next morning, after quitting the training camp and IRONMAN® racing again, I got up at 4:30 a.m. Still more asleep then awake, I drove fifty miles into the city and went for a one-mile open water swim before work. That morning, for the first time, I just flew through the water. I didn't zigzag, hyperventilate, or burn out like I had in every previous swim. I don't know why I went for that long swim on the first day after quitting training, especially since I was supposed to be enjoying my summer vacation.

The next day, I left work early, drove to Afton, and biked one of the most extreme hills in Minnesota ten times from bottom to top and back down. I didn't cramp up, slow down, or bite the dust like I had on other training rides that summer. The following day, Wednesday, I swam two miles in open water with out issue and Thursday I ran five miles - fast. On Saturday morning, Kathy went to Madison to train on the IRONMAN Wisconsin course, and for some dumbass reason I went with her. This time, I finished the entire 112-mile bike course alongside my wife.

I had turned a corner somewhere along the way and had that breakthrough moment that you sometimes read about and oftentimes pray for. Boom went the dynamite! I finally was able to bike around the Madison course.

On the drive home from Madison, the pieces finally started coming together. If I kept hydrated, I could keep going. If I kept my calories at 350 per hour, I wouldn't hit the wall. If I didn't eat processed sugar, I wouldn't get dizzy. If I kept up with my electrolytes, I wouldn't get cramps. If I crashed, I only needed to drop my heart rate for ten minutes and I would recover.

Otter, eagle, possum. If I swam like an otter, corkscrewing my shoulders, making my body profile streamlined and sleek, and slipping through the water, I could swim faster and expend less energy. If I pedaled up the hills in a low gear, not expending a lot of energy, and then coasted down them, swooshing like an eagle, I would retain more energy for the run. If I could just keep on the run long enough until the sun went down, I knew I could recover lost strength from the day and, like the possum, keep moving through the night.

Otter, eagle, possum. That became my mantra. The otter, eagle, possum strategy was born.

I immediately worked my training schedule up to an insane level, biking over 200 miles, swimming four miles, and running a half marathon in one week.

I don't know what happened to cause this turn around. In hindsight, the only explanation is that all the small lessons and big training done over the past year had finally caught up. Like some kind of weird miracle, I was finally able to go the distance in training. Could I do it in a race?

Self Talk

Self talk is probably the biggest differentiator between first and last place in an endurance race. While it is impossible to control the weather, the course, the crowds, other racers, or your genetics, you can control how you think about yourself. How you think about yourself ultimately controls how you perform. In a triathlon, self talk takes on a stronger meaning than it does in other sports, as the racer is alone without any feedback other than their thoughts for most of the day.

Part of the turnaround that took me from average Joe to an IRONMAN® athlete was just plain getting my head around the fact that I was capable of finishing the race.

Heart Attack and Die

While it seemed like I could build myself up to finish the swim and bike, I was very worried about dying on the course before I could finish the run. Not dying as in going slow, but dying as in getting carried off the course by the coroner. The reason for this was an incorrect self-diagnosis of a bad heart, compounded by the fact that my mom had just passed away due to cardiac failure.

When the training picked up mid-year, I got extreme chest pains during exercise. These pains would subside a few hours after the exercise stopped. Months later, I learned that they were being caused by an out-of-alignment rib, which could be fixed by a simple chiropractic adjustment.

Before finding this out, I thought that I only had a few more months to live. I thought about mentioning this to my wife, but she had already raised concerns about my health, so I did not want to add another issue to her list. Her solution was to increase my life insurance!

I thought about seeing a doctor but suspected that they would tell me not to start the race because of the chest pains and that I would have to go through some wild kind of cardiac surgery.

Ultimately, I decided to man up and run the race. If I died, it seemed like it would happen early on in the swim, and then at least I wouldn't have to struggle to the finish.

Time Management

Time management is easy for the triathlete. Work, sleep, eat, train. Everything else is irrelevant. Friends get tired of not hearing from you and stop calling you. Bills stack up in the corner of the kitchen, not because you don't have money to pay them, but because it is not a priority to get them paid. The dog loses weight because you constantly forget to feed him. Your car doesn't get washed.

The only two times that you eat are when you are training and when you are at work. You never have time to sit down with friends outside of your schedule. In fact, you have to eat constantly to repair your body from the last day's training and prepare it for the upcoming training.

You eat everything you can get your hands on and nothing seems off limits. One time I had to chuckle at myself as I was eating cookies while sitting on the crapper. It had seemed like a good way to multi-task. Some nights I would raid the kitchen at 2:00 a.m. and bump into Kathy, who would be standing in front of the kitchen cupboard, blank faced and in her underwear, jamming food in her mouth.

You piggyback any social event with a bike, run, or swim— or often times all three. Eventually you break the twenty-hour-a-week training barrier and begin to feel deep Catholic-style guilt if you miss a training session.

Sleep is hard to get during training. I began to find it in unusual places. I fell asleep in meetings at least once a week during the summer due to exhaustion from the previous day's training. Several people confronted me about it, and it became quite comical to some people whenever I snapped my head back awake. I also fell asleep several times at stop lights while driving.

The one place I found it hard to sleep was in bed after a hard day's training. Kath and I called this runner's anxiety, and many other athletes experienced this as well. The symptoms of this disorder include lying awake at two in the morning staring at the ceiling as your legs keep twitching you awake.

You realize at some point that the training is dark, meaningless, and self-serving, but you blow off everything that is important in life and keep training anyways. Alcoholics are not diagnosed based on the amount they drink. Rather, it is based on whether business or personal relationships are impacted by the person's behavior or if a person's physical health is being affected by the amount they drink. By these measures, the training required is a disease of the worst magnitude. All that is important is feeding the training addiction, getting the next adrenaline fix, and figuring out a way to do more, go farther, go faster, and get higher than the time before.

Eventually you become what you are training to be: a lean, mean racing machine. The only thing bigger than your calves and shoulders is your ego. No ride, run, or swim is too much. Your perspective on runners is that they are underachievers because they don't swim and bike. Cyclists become second-class athletes who can't swim. Swimmers are people who don't bike. Pride and fulfillment can only come from mastering the multi sport—swim, bike, run.

Not only do you see it when you look in the mirror, but also in the faces of the friends you make along the way. Like a high school graduating class, the athletes who are left by the end of the summer are jolly green giants, ready to take on the world. Many talked not only about finishing the upcoming IRONMAN® race but tackling several more after that. The deep creases in their sunburned faces spoke of the hours they had spent on the road and in the water. Their shoulders are so big that their hands rotate slightly inward. Pot bellies are replaced with lean abs by summer's end. Calf muscles bulge from skinny ankles. Pants that are tight on the thighs are loose in the waist.

Eventually you are ready, and there are no more training days left. Eventually the gun goes off, and you start the race. It was now September. We were done training and ready to become IRONMAN finishers.

September 7— Packing for IRONMAN® Wisconsin

Packing for the race is part of the adventure. For people who love piddling with gear and fussing with gadgets, this is a magical time. I downright hate the anxiety that race packing gives me and inevitably forget something major every time I pack.

For ten months, Kath and I had been packing up our triathlon gear and heading out on the road. The Wednesday before hitting the road for the last time, I packed in record time and did not forget anything. This small miracle was a by-product of all of the training trips we had done.

I will share a few packing tips, most of which we learned the hard way. First and foremost, get one big bag that can contain four smaller bags. I use a hockey bag, but any soft-side bag will work. In this larger bag, place one bag for swimming, one for biking, one for running, and one for post-race clothes. In each of my individual sport bags, I pack one ziplock bag with my nutrition and another with my pills.

One last time we took the dogs to the kennel and hooked up with a neighbor who would care for the cat, farm, and house. I lined up help to care for the chickens and the livestock and packed up the car.

On the Way to the Race

On the way to the race, Kath and I drove four hours out of the way to rural northern Wisconsin to meet my immediate family and their spouses at the family cabin. The cabin was located on top of a large outcropping of granite boulders. A crystal clear river cut through the moss-covered red rocks. Tall, skinny birch and aspen grew in a thick forest on the banks. The cabin was ground zero for many of our family experiences.

My grandparents had bought the land in the mid-seventies and moved a trailer house on it as a getaway for the extended family. It was our redneck version of the Kennedys' Camelot and in our grandparents' eyes, we were all going to be future presidents.

Us kids grew up in the river, swimming, tubing, fishing, and hunting the deer and ducks that lived on its banks. The parents hung out in the cabin, cleaning, cooking, relaxing, and keeping us from killing ourselves. As we got older, the adventures became bigger and the toys became louder. By the time we were teenagers, we were whipping through the woods on our motorcycles and drinking beer by the case.

All of us treated the river cabin as a physical and mental destination. My mom requested in her will to have her ashes spread there.

Once Kath and I got to the river, we got in canoes, paddled out in the water, and sprinkled my mom's ashes in the Wolf River in front of the cabin. My sisters threw flower petals in the water as my mom's ashes sank to the bottom. The petals floated past us quickly, like the short time that it seemed we had with my mom.

My mom was full of wisdom, strength, and humor. Wow, I really miss her.

It was kind of fun to be back together canoeing with my father, brother, sisters, and in-laws, and memories of being young washed away the sadness of the day.

As always, we had to cut the day short due to the green monster of the triathlon schedule. We jumped back into the car and drove four hours to Madison to check in our equipment and start the final race countdown.

Athlete Check-In and Pre-Race Expo— The Pretender

We drove from the cabin to Madison in relative silence, occasionally sharing memories of my mom. We parked the car at the Monona Terrace and walked into the expo to register and pick up equipment for the race. In my head, I knew I was going to drop out of the race and that being at the expo was nothing more than a lie. I was not a finisher, so why should I even be a starter?

The waves in Lake Monona were huge that day, and the rumor was that the fire department had to rescue two swimmers who went out to practice on the course.

Additionally, I had never run more than sixteen miles at a time this summer, and that time was a horrible experience. Worse, I knew what to expect with the bike course and realized that the odds of an over-the-hill, less-than-adequately-trained, diabetic athlete like me finishing the race were slim.

There was really no way that I could pull off the race. There was only one small glimmer of hope. Kathy's prediction seemed to be coming true—the weather forecast for race day called for no wind, no rain, low humidity, and cool temperatures. Maybe, just maybe, I could pull it off and finish the race. Maybe I wasn't a pretender amongst contenders after all.

We met our daughter Anna and walked into the pre-race expo in fairly good spirits. Once inside, we navigated a gauntlet of process and administration to get officially checked in. One step required us to weigh in on their scale. The reason for this was that if you lost five percent of your body weight on race day, you would be removed from the course for safety reasons. I came in at 205 pounds. I had lost 40 pounds since the New York Marathon and felt like I was ready to race at that weight.

We racked our bikes in a staging area in the parking garage of the Monnona Terrace. The bikes were ordered by their owners' bib numbers. The pro athletes had the best positions in the parking lot. I was parked in the back with the other 45-year-old guys. Each athlete was handcuffed with a blue hospital-style wristband on one arm that had his or her number on it. In order to get in and out of the bike corral, you had to be wearing one of these blue bands, and the number on the band needed to match the number that was pasted on the bike.

Athletes' Dinner— Mike Reilly

One of the rituals that veteran triathletes had recommended participating in was the pre-race pasta dinner. Several thousand athletes and their supporters packed into one huge room in the Monona Terrace for dinner, pre-race discussion, and a short presentation from Mr. IRONMAN® himself, Mike Reilly. Mike was the master of ceremonies for the night and is the announcer for the race. His voice is famous for announcing the names of the finishers over the loudspeaker as they cross the finish line: *"JOHN SMITH, YOU ARE AN IRONMAN!"*

Mike's proclamation is something you carry with you for life. It will likely be listed in your eulogy along with the family you've raised, the college you attended, and the military service you completed.

I once was told that when Mike sees you coming up to the line and calls your name, you are transformed from an ordinary athlete into the extraordinary finisher, and you get a hall pass on ever being called boring.

We had one more opportunity to bump into people who we had met in the previous eighteen months of training. All of them were wearing the athlete's blue wristband. I also made a few new friends, as there is always something to chat about when you meet a fellow ultra distance triathlete.

Mike put on a great show, introducing the youngest athletes, the oldest athlete, the biggest loser, and the athlete with the most children. I was both amazed and encouraged by huge differences among the athletes. Ages ranged from 18 to 73. They introduced the oldest female competitor, who was 68 and looked like she was 18. The oldest male was 73—he would end up beating me by almost two hours. The biggest loser had lost almost 100 pounds during his training.

The other remarkable thing was the varied body sizes and shapes. Tall, short, thick, and thin, it was hard to look at some people and believe they were athletes, much less full-distance triathletes. The one thing that we all had in common, though, was that we had gone through a hell of a lot of training to get to the starting line, and with that, we were all in remarkable shape.

Mike ended the night by saying that he looked forward to announcing all of our names as IRONMAN® finishers when we crossed the finish line. Slowly, over the course of the evening, my confidence had risen. I began to think that I could finish the race.

Rules

I have a deep respect for the legends and rituals surrounding IRONMAN® triathlons. With that said, IRONMAN races have more rules governing the safety and competitiveness of the event than just about any other sport I am aware of. The rules were covered in a thirty-minute session that night at dinner. Some are necessary, while others seem ridiculous.

One rule states that you have to pass slower bikers on the left, then immediately move to the right. Failure to do this results in a two-minute penalty. Judges on motorcycles actually buzz around the bike course looking for infractions. This rule is in place to keep riders from drafting off each other and, in theory, improves the competitiveness of the event.

They actually have penalty tents where unlucky racers who get caught violating one rule or another have to sit and watch others go by. In my opinion, some of the rules should be removed from the event. For example, I was penalized four minutes one year when my teenage daughter ran alongside me for a few blocks.

iPods are banned completely from the sport. In my opinion, personal music devices are not bad and don't promote chaos or a present a safety hazard on the run. I understand not biking and swimming with them, but seriously, rock and roll may have brought down the Berlin wall but it isn't a threat to the 140.6.

Another stupid rule is that kids cannot cross the finish line with their parents. I have heard that in some races if your kids cross the line with you, they will take away your finisher's medal. Horse shit! Allowing kids to come across the finish line with their parents could promote the next generation of the sport, and that is worth any safety issues it causes.

Yet another example of a dumbass rule is that an athlete cannot accept ice or pop on the course from anyone who is not officially associated with the race. So for instance, if your mom sees that you are overheating, she cannot pass you a cupful of ice. Wow.

These rules were written by people who, in my opinion, want to suck all of the fun out of the event. If any race officials are reading this, I would encourage them to revaluate these rules and revise them to make the sport more enjoyable for the average or, in my case, less-than-average person.

Race Morning

I downed two sleeping pills and jumped into the hotel bed at 8:00 p.m. the night before the race. As I laid awake in bed, anxiety over the next morning refused to leave my head. I could not help but think about warriors in Afghanistan that very evening laying awake and suffering from the anxiety of going into combat the next morning. Certainly though, my anxiety was a first-world problem, and I felt a little twinge of weeniness when I compared myself to America's warriors.

Because of the sleeping pills, I slept pretty well and woke up at 3:30 a.m. after the chemical haze wore off. The sleeping pills had been in my race plan for many months prior and I had actually made them part of my training regime. Getting this good night's sleep was important, as I knew I would be awake for the next twenty-four hours.

Kath and I had actually thought about getting separate hotel rooms but ended up just getting a king-sized bed to ensure that we got plenty of sleep. Not that I am one to kiss and tell, but if I was, there would have been nothing to tell about that night, other than dreams of the race to come.

Kath and I got ready in the morning without saying much to each other. At this point, the pre-race routine was pretty much wrote. This is one of the residual benefits of doing several practice races. Also, most of our gear was already staged on the course, so all we really needed to do was fill up our water bottles and special needs bags and drive to the course.

This is a good time to talk about special needs and transition bags. The IRONMAN® event organizers provide five big bags. These bags are labeled as follows: morning clothes, swim-to-bike transition, bike-to-run transition, run special needs, and bike special needs. The race organizers take accountability for the gear in these bags and they are placed at strategic points in the race. Runners put extra clothes, medicine, food, and drinks in them. This reduces the chaos of carrying all that gear and improves the quality and conformity of the race.

In the morning clothes bag, you place the gear that you wear down to the swim and then presumably will change back into when you leave the course.

In the swim-to-bike transition bag, you put your helmet, shoes, socks, shirt, and shorts (if you didn't wear them on the swim), sunglasses, pills, and anything else required to get you through the bike course.

In the bike special needs bag you put fresh socks and maybe a jacket. I also packed a Coke, a Snickers bar, and gummy bears. This bag is placed at mile 56 of the bike course, the halfway point.

In the bike-to-run transition bag, I put dry socks, shorts, a hat, and a shirt. Also, my cell phone, a credit card in case of emergency, another Snickers bar, gummy bears, and another Coke.

In the run transition bag, I put pills, eye drops, sunglasses, and a lot of hope, because I knew that if I got to that point I would get to the end of the race.

You will notice that I put a lot of sugar in my race day plan, especially considering that I am pre-diabetic. This was a conscious plan to give me the go-for-broke energy I would need to get me through the grueling distance one last time. In hindsight, this definitely caused many of the day's nutritional ups and downs.

Pre-Race Frenzy

My sister Jayne picked us up at the hotel and drove to the Mono-na Terrace at 4:00 a.m. that morning. We were all silent. At the terrace, floodlights were turning the dark morning into daylight. Everyone was walking around like zombies as they went through checklists and performed final preparations. Everyone's preparation was slightly different: walking here, packing this, pumping tires, checking gear. But no one's path seemed like it crashed them into anyone else's. It was like some kind of choreographed pre-race frenzy.

Moths were darting in and around the bright lights powered by smoking diesel generators. It was still midnight dark where the floodlights weren't shining and we walked through this surreal environment to get our bodies marked.

Body marking is a unique triathlon ritual. In this process, your race number is written in permanent marker on your arms and calves like some kind of tribal tattoo. Mine was 1835 and Kath's was 131. I also took a marker and wrote my mom's name ("JUDY") in big letters on my the inside of my left forearm and "USMC" on my right. I figured that looking down at these body markings would give me strength during the race. It did, and I needed it.

The Swim Start— Peeing, Praying, and Panicking

The morning slipped away from us way too fast and the dawn replaced the dark. It was time. Kath and I kissed and she walked into the water ahead of me at approximately 6:30 a.m. to line up for the swimming start. Her strategy was to get into the water early and warm up. I went into the water at 6:50 a.m. My strategy was to expend as little energy as possible dog paddling around at the deep water start.

As I treaded water with the 2500 other swimmers, I focused on my race plan and took one last pee into my wet suit. That was the last pee I would take for almost twenty-four hours. My biggest fears during the race were that I would either die of a heart attack during the swim or squirt liquid crap all over myself on the run. I was hoping for the former, because if I died early, I wouldn't have to worry about the hassle of changing poopy shorts during the marathon.

You would think that at this point I would have said some kind of prayer about competing, finishing, or the safety of myself and the other athletes. I was raised Catholic and became a born again Christian in 1996 at 3:00 a.m. one crystal clear, bitter cold, Minnesota, January morning. While on a snowmobile trip, looking up at all of the stars in the universe, it made sense to give my life over to Jesus.

Since then, my faith has ebbed and flowed. At no point in the race did I ask God to help me finish, or for any other favor. Unfortunately, more than a few times, the only thing that I came close to doing was cursing him. There was this comforting feeling I had, though, when I was floating in the water at the starting line, that he was with me.

There is no question that God gave us a perfect day to race. 70° F water, 70° F air temperature, no rain, very little wind, and negligible humidity. It just doesn't get better than that. At many points in the race, I could feel God running beside me, and I am absolutely, 100 percent confident that he carried me across the finish line that day.

There were 2500 people bobbing up and down in about 8 feet of murky water at this point. Most were dressed in full-length black wet suits, swim caps, and goggles. We were tightly packed together into an area of about two acres. The surface was dead calm except for the ripples from the swimmers treading water. There was a small amount of chitchat, but otherwise no one was saying much. The sun was coming up and there was a slight fog in the air.

The crowd was onshore about a hundred yards away, and a DJ was blasting techno and pop music. The top floor of the Monona Terrace was lined with people watching the spectacle of the swim start. I was cool as a cucumber floating in the water, ready to bring the race on. For the first time that day, I heard the ever-present clanging of cow bells coming from shore. The cow bell is the unmistakable trademark of the IRONMAN® Wisconsin race.

A few minutes before seven, "The Star Spangled Banner" started blasting across the loudspeakers, and as usual I had to choke back tears while it was being played—like every ex-Marine. Then the DJ cranked up the volume of the PA system even louder and jammed U2's "A Beautiful Day." The cannon went off and BOOM, the swimmers zoomed out. When I say zoomed, I mean we zoomed!

Race Start
140.6 Miles Left—
17 Hours until Cut-off

The closest thing I can think of to compare a triathlon shotgun swim start to is the excitement of a state fair dirt track stock car race start. The blur of speed, racers bumping into each other, and everyone jockeying for position causes quite a commotion. The first hundred yards went well, and in the next hundred yards I started climbing on other swimmers' backs as I accelerated past them. Within 300 hundred yards, I had been kicked in the face, back, stomach, and arms as I passed people and people passed me. I started getting pissed off that I was being beat up so bad and quickly learned how to use my hands and feet to defend myself. I purposely popped a guy in the head as payback for punching me in the face a few times. Hell, he didn't care, so neither did I. The race was on!

At the first corner of the essentially square course, the group came to a stop and bunched up as 2500 people tried to hang a left. A woman climbed up my back and onto my shoulders then ripped off my goggles. I grabbed her hand and flipped her off my back, made sure she wasn't drowning, and pushed her away. We were jammed front to back, butt cheeks to belly buttons, totally floating upright in ten feet of water. We were like too many spoons crammed into the silverware container of a dishwasher. Many of the people started mooing like cows (an IRONMAN® Wisconsin race tradition), mocking the absurdity of the situation. I just laughed at the incredible chaos. I found a small window of empty water off to my left and started swimming again. By the second turn, the crowd thinned out and I was able to stretch out my stroke and make time.

As we passed course buoys and other swimmers I was amazed by how fast I was going. By the time I made the first lap around, I knew I was making a personal record time. I learned that by staying to the inside of the pack, there were less swimmers competing for open water, and I was getting pulled along in the wake of the people in front of me. It really seemed like there was an inside groove to the course, as all I found was choppy water when I veered to the outside of the pack.

I was slipping through the water in my wet suit just like the otter on Kathy's lake.

It seemed like no time at all had passed, and I had nearly completed the second lap and was on the home stretch. I paused for a moment and took in the sight of the crowd on the shore. The crowd was loud, the music was pumping, and cow bells were clanging. I stuck my foot down and it finally touched bottom. I had made it to the end of the 2.4-mile swim. Like a duck, I waddled my way out of the water. On shore was a large clock that showed my time: 1:26. One hour and twenty-six minutes.

My vision was still a little cloudy from the water that leaked through my goggles and sloshed into my eyes. This couldn't possibly have been my time. I started running numbers in my head, trying to understand how I could post such a fast time. I had planned for a 1:50 swim, two hours max. How could this be? I thought to myself as I dropped down on the shore in front of gorgeous blonde stripper.

Well, not the pole-dancing kind of stripper, but a volunteer wet suit stripper. In one yank, she ripped off my wet suit, wrapped it up, and stuffed it into my arms. I winked at her and gave a thumbs-up to say thanks. Now barefoot and wearing nothing but my bike shorts and a smile, I ran up the helix to the transition area in the Monona Terrace to get into my biking gear.

I had planned for a one-hour and fifty-minute swim and ended up coming in at 1:26. I couldn't believe it. I owe the fast time to three things:

My coach told me to focus on cutting a straight line by sighting the buoys every fifth stroke. I did, and it worked.

My friend told me that the enormous wake of 2500 swimmers all going in the same direction would pull me along. It did.

My head told me that the faster I got out of the water, the earlier I could get on with my day. And I did.

I wasn't anxious and I didn't hyperventilate in the water. This perfect swim was due to the large amount of outdoor training that we did to prepare for the race. Also, while many of the other swimmers complained about getting kicked, punched, pulled, and pushed in the water, I just focused on swimming and did not care about what everyone else was doing.

Much of my family was waiting at the transition area and cheering with the thousands of other spectators watching the race. I flew through the transition from swim to bike as fast as I had flown through the water. My secret to success this time was to wear my bike shorts under my wet suit, a lesson I had learned at the IRONMAN® 70.3® Racine race.

Bike Start, 138.6 Miles Left— 15 Hours, 36 Minutes until Cut-off

I ran next to my bike, pushing it out of the transition area with hundreds of other athletes. Our bike shoes, not meant for running, click-clacked on the cement floor of the parking garage. My eyes were big with exhilaration and my knuckles were white and pruned from spending an hour and a half in the water.

I heard a chirp when I crossed the timing pad, signaling the system's recognition of my timing chip. I was now at the beginning of the bike race. I swung my leg over the cross tube and mounted my Cannondale. I rolled down the helix from the parking garage and onto the street with both hands on the brakes. I was tightly packed in with other athletes and our brakes squeaked as we descended carefully to avoid colliding.

Once out of the helix and on the street, the wind flowed over my body and dried the last drops of water from Lake Monona off my skin. My endorphins were maxed and I was so pumped up by my rocket fast swim time that when I started out on the bike course I felt invincible and lucent—two things that had never happened before. Was it possible that I might actually have a good finishing time?

The whirl of the tires and the mashing of gears was interrupted by a *tink, tink, tink* as my electrolyte pills bounced out of the little storage box on my bike and tumbled onto the pavement. This time, I turned around and went back and got them, another lesson learned from Racine.

As I headed out of town, I snacked on the Hostess apple pie that I had strategically crammed underneath my bike seat the night before. It was a reward for getting through the swim. *Could it get better than this?* I wondered to myself.

First Bike Loop 120 Miles Left— 14 Hours until Cut-off

I was in a large pack of maybe a hundred bikers, and I thought that I would stick with them for the first half of the bike race before making my move when the pack slowed down. My confidence was high after the swim, and I was going to play it smart and pace myself for the first fifty-six miles. We weren't going very fast—maybe seventeen miles per hour—and I had a chance to talk to people as we pedaled out of town. Spirits were very high and I traded compliments, insults, and encouragements with the other riders.

By mile ten, the pace had picked up, and so did the hills. I was careful not to chase the pack, and while many of the bikers moved up to a twenty-mile-per-hour pace, I changed gears and dialed it back to about fifteen miles per hour. The first few hills were like a slap in the face. I could feel my thighs tense up with each hill, and my endurance and confidence were slowly dripping out of me like the sweat on my forehead.

A coach once told me that your endurance is like a book of matches. With each challenge, such as a hill, a match is lit. When all of the matches in the book are lit, your endurance is burned out and you can't get it back. I had found this to be good advice, but by managing my caloric intake and heart rate, I could actually bounce back from the brink of bonking. This was another lesson learned during the long hours of training that summer.

A short 30 miles into the 112 mile bike segment, I was noticeably beginning to wear down. I was sweating profusely, my head was swimming, my heart rate was peaking, and my fingers were swollen. The problem-solving part of my brain kicked in, and I searched my memory banks for the solution to these problems.

My self-diagnosis was that, in all of the excitement of the previous hours, I skimped on my nutrition plan. So, I popped two electrolyte pills and guzzled twelve ounces of water to counteract the fluid loss from sweating. I also wolfed down an energy bar to get my empty stomach fueled back up. I dialed my pace back even further to slow my heart rate. I needed to get my strength back to finish the remaining ninety miles, and these were the tools to fuel the engines.

I looked at the words "USMC" and "JUDY" scrawled on my inner forearms. I was refueled with both nutrition and determination.

The orange autumn sun was starting to climb in the midmorning sky, and so was the mercury in the thermometer. The first major challenge of the race presented itself, a sweeping uphill into Mt Horab. I slipped the bike into the lowest gear and spun the crank quickly to motor to the top of the hill. Several racers passed me on the grinding uphill, but for the most part I kept my position. When I got to the top, I felt more depleted than I had in previous training rides this far into the course. At that moment, a little anxiety crept into my head and I began to think that the day might turn ugly.

Bike Mile 40— Cross Plains Water Stop

Once on the top of the hill, I began the fifteen-mile ride into Cross Plains. Kath and I called this section the razor back, as the extreme downhill path was punctuated with about a dozen quick, steep, rolling hills. At the top of one of them was a lonely sign that had been placed by a spectator. It read "you need to finish the course to get the tattoo." This made me smile, as I wanted to get an IRONMAN® tattoo after finishing the race. After getting through the razor back, we biked onto the relatively flat river bottom that hosts the town of Cross Plains.

On this half-mile-long stretch of the race, the bikers merge into a mostly single file line, slow down to about ten miles per hour and grab water and Gatorade bottles held out by volunteers. It is a high-excitement goat rodeo of un-choreographed activity. Missed bottles popped out of athletes' hands and flew in the air before skittering across the ground. Bikers swerved and jockeyed to avoid crashing into each other and dropped bottles on the course. The more aggressive riders tried to pass the slower riders in the choke point of the aid station. The ground was covered by a slick of water and Gatorade that had been spilled during the refueling process.

As I rolled past the first volunteer, I grabbed one bottle and quickly emptied it into my forward on-board water container. Without stopping, I threw the empty to the side of the road and grabbed another bottle from a second volunteer. I put this one into an empty bottle carrier on my bike. I kept rolling forward and grabbed one last water bottle then drained it over my head to cool myself off. In a minute I was clear of the aid station and back on the course.

We crossed over a railroad track and headed back out of the small town. Cow bells rang as we departed. The sound grew softer the farther we went, until eventually the excitement of the aid station was completely behind us. At this point, the road split down the middle of a dairy farm and the summery smells of cattle perfumed the air.

Bike Mile 46— Three Very Large Hills

Within two miles of the Cross Plains aid station, the second big hill appeared. Affectionately named Road Kill Hill, it was a sweeping half-mile-long, 150-foot vertical climb that was packed with spectators. I put my bike in the lowest gear and started spinning. Resisting the urge to stand up on the pedals until the last moment to conserve energy, I finally reached the top.

About two miles from the top of Road Kill Hill was the third big hill, called Tower Hill by the locals. Kath and I called it Bald Hill, as it looked a lot like my shaved head. This hill was a beast. It was a straight up 200-foot vertical in about a quarter-mile stretch without shade.

There was a guy dressed as a devil watching on the hill. He would run alongside athletes' bikes and poke them with his fake trident as they busted ass to pedal to the top. Another guy trotted alongside me wearing a big foam finger with "number one" printed on it. He was screaming in my face that I was number one. I looked at him in complete disbelief. I don't have any idea why someone would do that.

Cow bells were banging loudly. People were screaming. Even

weirder, at the top of the hill was a crowd of guys cross-dressed as cheerleaders and doing a cancan line dance. Fuck, it was an odd crowd of spectators along that part of the course.

Bike Mile 56— Race Within Your Box

The good news was that I had made it to the halfway point in the bike course. The bad news was that I was going way slower than expected. I had trained for a 7:30 total bike time, and reaching the halfway point had taken about four hours. Based on past experience, I knew that the second loop split time was never faster than the first loop's split. This meant that it would take me more than eight hours to finish. To make matters worse, my old enemy the sun was peaking, and I was tired, sore, cramping, grumpy, and lightheaded.

There was a special needs station at the halfway point, so I got off my bike and sat on a curb alongside the road. A volunteer told me to move because I was in a dangerous spot. I told her I couldn't. She looked me in the eyes with sympathy and smiled. She told me to wait there and took my number and said she would be right back with my special needs bag.

I had trained much further distances on much hotter days and had always been in better shape at this point in the course. Why this? Why now? The only thing that I could think of is that I had expended more energy than normal on the swim. I had to get that strength back somehow.

The volunteer brought me my special needs bag, and I could tell by the way that she was looking at me that I looked as rough as I felt. Deep in my special needs bag was a bottle of Coke. Not Diet Coke like the doctor told me pre-diabetics should drink, but real Coke with sugar. Score! I guzzled it down like a kid on a TV commercial. With that sixteen ounces of glucose and caffeine, I was instantly jolted back to life. Nothing like a Coke and a smile.

My thighs were tight and I was lightheaded and tipsy when I stood up. The volunteer tried to grab my arm as if she was afraid I was going to fall over. I politely thanked her and then brushed the dirt off my bike shorts from where I had sat down on the ground. The dirt stuck to the back of my wet spandex shorts like sugar on a peanut butter cookie. The front of my black shorts was covered with white salt from the sweat dripping off my body.

I buckled my helmet back onto my head, threw one leg over the cross bar, and mounted my bike. Other racers were whizzing past me. I tucked in behind them and headed out toward the last five big hills, many small ones, and fifty-six miles that were between me and the finish of the bike course.

Wait a minute. At the end of the bike course was the beginning of the marathon! How did that work? My head started reeling as I grasped the insanity of first the swim, then the bike, then the run. No way was I going to make it. I needed some tool or some trick to avoid dropping out of the race merely halfway into it.

I dug deep into my brain and thought about all of the advice the veteran racers had given me. Just then, a nugget of wisdom that had been shared with me by many racers and coaches popped into my head: *Race within your box*. What this meant was to set a short-term goal, focus on that, and not worry about the larger goal of getting to the finish. This tip finally made sense to me as I focused only on getting to Mt Horab, rather than finishing the bike course and then starting the marathon.

Second Time Around on the Bike Course—The Yo-Yo

I made it through the next sixteen miles at a slow but steady pace. When I saw the large sweeping hill heading up to Mt Horab, I dropped into my lowest gear and began the climb. It was about a half-mile extreme uphill with no protection from the merciless sun. Midway up the hill, I was moving forward at a snail's pace. For the first time that day, my stomach began to rumble and slosh. Luckily, when I got to the top of the hill there was a line of port-a-potties . I dismounted my bike and a volunteer quickly grabbed the handle bars to prevent it from tipping over and smacking the ground.

I whipped open the plastic door and dashed into the port-a-potty. It must have been over 100° F in there, and the smell wasn't too pleasant. I barely got my pants down when a volcano erupted. All of the nutrition I had accumulated during the first half of the day was now ejecting from my body into the plastic pot.

At that point, though, it really didn't seem to matter, as I was sitting in a comfortable spot and wasn't on my bike. Also, behind the closed door there was no expectation from the spectators or competition from the other riders. The port-a-potty was like my own personal Xanadu. While the smell in the port-a-potty was magnified by the intense heat, I just did not feel like getting off the throne. I dozed off for a minute of sleep for the first time that day. I was not in a hurry to leave my personal spa.

At some point, the reality of the locality slipped in, and while my tired legs wanted to keep sitting, I pulled up my spandex bike shorts and kicked open the door. It was race day, and I had business to do. The hot sun banged into me as I stepped back on the course.

The volunteer who was holding my bike looked at me like, *Really? You were in there an awfully long time.* She asked me if I was okay. I faked a smile, thanked her, and grabbed my bike. Before getting on it I popped two Imodium pills that I had packed for just this type of situation. They instantly put out the volcano that was rumbling in my stomach.

I set a goal of making it to the Cross Plains water stop fifteen miles ahead and pushed forward on my bike. The terrain between Mt Horab and Cross Plains was very hilly, with a lot of steep ups and downs. I knew what to expect from all of the training we had done and made it though the razor back roller coaster once again. When I got to Cross Plains the second time, there was cause to celebrate, as I was only twenty-five miles from the finish. The bad news was that those twenty-five miles contained four very large hills and numerous smaller ones. I got off my bike for the third time that day and sat on the curb for a minute.

It was highly unusual, but not illegal, for a racer to get off their bike and sit down. A dismounted biker was a trouble sign, and several volunteers walked up to ask if I was okay. I said that I was and laid back in the grass to catch my breath and collect my thoughts.

I did a quick mental inventory of my physical status and thought about the remaining twenty-five miles of cycling and twenty-six miles of running to go. It seemed unlikely that I could finish that distance, given my current run-down, ridden-hard condition. For the first time that day, the real possibility that I would not finish the race entered my mind.

I figured, though, that no matter what shape I was currently in, I still had to get my bike to the finish. So I popped a couple of electrolyte pills, washed them down with water, and squirted the rest of the water bottle down the back of my racing jersey. I jumped up, buckled up my helmet, and shuffled back to my bike. I was determined to bike my way to the finish at the Monona Terrace rather than quit the race and get driven back.

After ten minutes of riding, I was back on Road Kill Hill for the second time that day. I dropped my gears into the small ring in the front and the big ring in the back, giving me maximum climbing power. I picked up my pedaling cadence and began working my way to the top of the steep, sweeping hill. This time, though, my left hamstring locked up tight midway up the hill. My bike lost speed instantly and came to a stop for a moment before it started rolling backward.

Bike Mile 75— The Course Goes Uphill and the Rider Goes Down

Because my feet were clipped into my pedals, I lost balance and tumbled to the ground in a three point landing: hand first, shoulder second, hip last. Having fallen off my bike just the same way several times that year already, I had figured out how to do an Airborne Ranger kind of tuck and roll, so the fall didn't really hurt too badly. I struggled to my feet and stood up my bike.

What did hurt was the fact that my leg muscles were too tight to power the pedals. Worse, if I did get back on the bike at that spot, the steepest part of the hill, I had no momentum to get me rolling forward and I would likely fall over again as the bike slipped backward.

I decided to do the unthinkable and walked my bike up the remainder of the hill. It was hard to say at that point what hurt worse, the brutalized leg muscles or my broken pride. I walked my bike up the rest of the hill without looking any other competitors or spectators in the eye. As I walked, my leg muscles loosened up and my heart rate came back to normal. I mounted my Cannondale at the top of the hill and biked on to the next obstacle, just a few miles away, Tower Hill.

There was no chance that I could make it up Tower Hill the second time, so I unclipped midway up that monster to avoid falling over for the second time that day. This time, I walked with a look of defiance rather than dejection, as I knew I was getting closer to the finish. A few miles later, I had to climb yet one more large hill. This one we called 7711, for the address on the mailbox at the top of the hill, and this time I pumped all the way to the top, just to prove that I could still do it.

In retrospect, this show of force was probably a bad idea, as any strength that I had in my body was left on the hill. I rode the next ten miles into Verona at about fifteen miles per hour and hit the water stop by the school. They had a big ice machine there, so I put handfuls in my jersey and down the front of my spandex shorts in an attempt to cool down. This helped somewhat.

I was like an emotional and physical yo-yo at that point, one minute up, the next minute down. My heart rate, mood, vision, and body temperature were all swinging radically from one extreme to another. I was hitting a wall about every thirty minutes. I did whatever it took, whether eating, resting, or drinking, to bust through each wall and push ahead until I hit the next cycle hit me.

Bike Mile 100— The Darkest Hour

By mile 100, I was again in major trouble. My stomach was a mess, and I had stopped sweating. I was lightheaded, and my fingers were so swollen that they were the size of sausages. In addition, I had no power in my legs and was biking at an average speed of about twelve miles per hour.

I had finally reached the end of my endurance and couldn't go any farther. I found a small grouping of ten-foot-tall Scotch pine trees on the side of the road and pulled off. I hid my bike from the road and the race. I unsnapped my helmet and laid down in a bed of pine needles underneath the trees, using my helmet as a pillow. I quickly drifted off to sleep. My mind's eye was running wild and dream visions were rapidly flipping in my head.

I was asleep but awake at the same time. I could hear the other racers whizzing by me on their bikes, but I didn't care. Scenes of training and races and friends flipped quickly through my mind. Awake, then back asleep, then awake again. I was watching the clouds. They were big, white, puffy battleships sprinting across the blue autumn sky. Flies landed on my face and ants were climbing on my ankles to drink spilled Gatorade.

My thoughts were blank. I tripped in and out of consciousness. My throat was dry.

I looked down at my runner's watch. The battery in it had died at seven-and-a-half hours. I had been on the course much longer than planned. A steady stream of bikers kept moving past me on the road. I don't know how long I laid there. It seemed like hours, but I believe now that it was only a few minutes.

I couldn't understand where I was at or what my next steps were. I didn't have any big thoughts. I wasn't sure if I was asleep or awake. I got on my feet, then walked my bike onto the road. I felt like I was stone drunk. The horizon was sloshing from side to side, and my vision was hazy. The vertigo of the situation made me nauseous.

Racers were swooshing by me, darting for the finish. I swung one leg over the cross tube of the Cannondale and clipped my right foot into the pedal. I got forward motion, sat down, clipped in my left foot, and just slowly biked ahead.

With the forward motion came recognition of where I was, and then, like a bucket of water being splashed on me, my consciousness came back. Bikes were whizzing past me, so I gained speed and kept pace with them. I took a mental inventory and recognized my location from previous training rides. I figured that I was only five miles from the finish of the bike race.

I could do that!

And then a short 26.2-mile jog to the finish of the marathon. Like fuck I was going to do that!

The problem-solving component of my brain was back online, and it quickly took charge. The only plan that made sense was to bike back to the terrace, get my wallet and cell phone, and call it quits. I would call my sister, and she could pick me up and drive me back to the hotel. Better yet, I could call a cab. I now had a plan. All I had to do was make it the five miles back to the Terrace.

I couldn't even make it that far. At 110 miles into a 112-mile course, I pulled my bike over again and laid down in the median of a road outside the Madison convention center. Again, I lost consciousness and fell asleep. Again, I had no idea if I was out for one minute or five. I couldn't even bike the last two miles to quit the race. Fuck. I went back to sleep. Looking back at my times and doing simple math, I think I was only asleep for about one or two minutes each time I laid down. At the time, though, it seemed like I was out for hours.

A few riders passed me. There were not a lot of people left on the bike course. I watched them whiz by. I stood up, buckled on my helmet, and shoved off the curb into the road. The remaining two miles had a lot of twists and turns. I started to feel a little better and then saw the Monona Terrace. I didn't celebrate. There was no joy in quitting a race before it was over. I did feel relief, though, that the day was done and that I would be sleeping in the hotel bed soon.

The last fifty yards of the bike course were straight up an inclined parking ramp helix into the second floor parking garage of the Monona Terrace. What a cruel trick by the course planners this was, to end the course on a tight, twisting uphill. How in goodness' name would I be able to do this? Unbelievably, I made it up the helix in low gear with no problem. Goodness had nothing to do with it, though. I cursed loudly the whole way up while standing on the pedals. Once at the top, I rode my bike over the timing pad that stood at the bike course finish and my time chip chirped.

Crowds of spectators were screaming. Cow bells were ringing. A volunteer handler immediately grabbed my bike from me and ran it to the bike rack. Another volunteer grabbed me under the arm and whisked me off the cement floor and into the changing area. My legs were wobbly, but somehow I made it through the door to the men's changing room.

Transition From Bike to Run

Once I was in the changing area, another handler shoved me down into a folding chair and took off my shoes while a third volunteer simultaneously grabbed my transition bag. Being one of the last into the transition area, I had my own dedicated staff of volunteers helping me. This is quite different for the athletes that came into transition mid-pack who may have had a tough time finding helping hands. Pretty soon the volunteers had me standing up in dry running clothes and were pushing me out the door and into the street. I really didn't have time to think about what I was doing. Like a professional pit crew at an Indy race, the handlers got their driver changed over and back out on the track.

I reached into my pocket and found pay dirt—my cell phone. My plan was perfectly executed. I was going to step out of the Terrace, quit the race, and then slip off into the crowd and disappear. I could then call my sister and get a ride back to the hotel. The horror of this beast was over. I was done.

A Good Plan Goes Bad— Marathon Mile 1

Unfortunately, the marathon course was lined with cattle grates and a thick layer of spectators, so it was impossible for me to break loose from the grip of the race. As fate would have it, I had to walk for around a mile to get out from behind the fence that held the spectators out and the participants in.

The grates wound around the capitol building and out onto State Street. The crowd was thick. People were cheering. The sights and sounds were overwhelming. The smell of carnival food—greasy french fries, coney dogs, and deep-fried cheese curds—filled the air. Had the circus come to town? A young female spectator made eye contact with me and asked how I was doing. All I could do was stare at the ground. She yelled, "Looking strong!" and shook her cow bell. Precisely one year before, I had seen a guy not too unlike me crying his eyes out at this point. The irony of the moment wasn't lost on me.

At the one mile marker, I saw my family. Not just my dad, brothers, sisters, and kids, but cousins and brides and aunts and uncles and nieces and nephews, all there to cheer me on. I was absolutely overwhelmed by seeing them and stopped walking to talk. They were somewhat encouraging but also very sarcastic about my slow pace, so I started to jog, making it to mile two before I started to walk again.

Marathon Mile 2– Disbelief

Mile two. No shit. Mile two. I couldn't believe I had come so far. What the fuck was I doing? Was I dreaming? Thirty minutes ago, I had been too tired to bike another mile, and now I had just run and walked two miles. Maybe I could make it to mile three. I put my head down and started to run one light pole, walk three, then run two light poles, walk two, and then run four, walk one. Twelve minutes passed, then thirteen minutes. I was now at the mile three marker.

It was somewhat remarkable to me that my body had once again broken through a wall and bounced back enough to get me to the next mile. This time, though, an even more remarkable thing had happened: my mind had bounced back as well.

The great Vince Lombardi once said whether you think you can win or whether you think you are going to lose, you are right. Lombardi was also quoted as saying that winners don't quit and quitters don't win. I wasn't going to win the race, but there seemed to be a slim and growing possibility that I might finish it.

Runners have to be very comfortable with the thoughts in their own heads and control their self talk. They need to get comfortable with controlling their own inner demons. In other sports, teams come together and build plays. There is plenty of conversation in between innings, quarters, or periods. There is no team or ball to pass in a triathlon. There are no complicated plays. It is all on you and in you.

Every minute is an internal struggle. Do I really want to do this? Do I want to quit? Do I have what it takes to finish? A triathlon is as much mental as it is physical. Some athletes actually hire a sports psychologist in addition to a conditioning coach.

I decided to neither commit to finishing nor take the leap and quit. I wasn't going to push the panic button and walk off the course as planned. Rather, I was just going to see if I could suck it up and make it another mile.

Marathon Mile 3— Clydesdale Down

At mile three I saw a guy who had passed me on his bike while I was lying down in the trees. He was a big boy like myself, Clydesdale class, easily 230 pounds, if not more. He was lying in the grass grasping his calf. There was a look of severe pain on his face. I couldn't think of anything to say, so I smiled, gave him a thumbs-up and kept moving. I found out later that he didn't finish the race.

I was clearly moving forward and was able to run for four or five minutes at a time before my head started to swim and my heart started to pound. When this happened, I would walk for a minute or two with my hands on my hips, gulping air and cooling off before picking up the pace and running again.

Marathon Mile 4— Where is the Possum?

At about mile four, in a light bulb moment, it occurred to me that the possibility of making it to the finish was growing. After all, I was following my strategy. I had swum like an otter and biked like an eagle, and if I could just hold on for the sun to go down, the possum in me would come out and I could run and walk to the finish.

Yeah, seriously, I told myself that. I must have been delirious, because as the geek in me woke up and looked at his watch, I realized that no matter how fast I ran I would not make it to the finish line before the cut-off time.

I needed a short-term goal to get my mind off the enormity of finishing the whole marathon. As the cliché goes, the way to eat an elephant is one bite at a time. I already had four miles behind me. Maybe I could make it to the halfway point in the marathon. I set a goal of making it to the turnaround point, the end of the first loop, at mile 13.1.

Marathon Miles 5 to 7— Camp Randal Stadium

I kept moving, one foot in front of the other, left, right, left, and soon the five-mile marker had come and gone. At that point, the course took a loop around the running track in Camp Randall Stadium. I made it a goal to run around the whole quarter mile track. And I did! I exited the stadium and the course headed out toward the lake.

At about mile seven, a course official told me that if I didn't hurry I wouldn't make the cut-off. I had no reasoning skills left, but I wondered if this meant I was possibly on pace to make the finish in time.

The sun's angry heat was burning out as it slowly sunk in the orange autumn sky. The coolness of the night was quickly filling in the gaps left behind by the day. As each degree of heat fell off the thermometer, I knew my chances of completing the race increased. If I could only hang on for four more hours.

One of the many rules in IRONMAN® racing is that you cannot receive outside assistance during the race. Depending on the assistance, you may get a few minutes added to your time or you may be disqualified altogether. My brother and sister started switching off pacing me. Technically this was considered outside assistance, and I would have been penalized if I were caught by a race official. At that moment, though, I was just glad to have the company and thought that the reward of their conversation far outweighed the risk of getting caught.

As we slowly plodded along, we talked about things from our past, our recently deceased mom, anything but the race. As the race progressed, I went from walking four units and running one to running four and walking one. There were actually a few miles where I ran the whole thing.

Marathon Mile 8— In the Dark of the Night

At about mile eight, I saw Kath. She was approximately six miles ahead of me and was coming back on her first loop of the course as I was heading out on mine. She looked very strong and, as usual, she had a swarm of guys running around her and was chatting them all up. Madison is a double loop course, so you get to see runners ahead of you as they pass by going the other direction. I was very happy that she was still alive and moving.

The sun was now gone, and the blackness of night embraced us with its refreshing breeze. The faster athletes had already finished the race and were probably back at their hotel rooms asleep. Some athletes were being swept from the course and sent home by race officials. They were too slow to meet the minimum cut-off time, so they were marked DNF (Did Not Finish) and bussed to the finish. I was still on the course, and the possum in me was alive in the darkness.

I did the math, and I could not add up a way that I would get to the finish line before the midnight cut-off time. But I kept going anyway. One foot in front of the other, one breath at a time. I got into an argument with my brother, who was running alongside me. He said that if I could just keep the same pace for the next sixteen miles, I could finish in time. I didn't believe him.

I thought that he was playing some kind of mind trick on me to keep me going. But the officials hadn't removed me from the course yet, so I must have been okay. He must have been right.

I passed other runners every now and then. We were a straggling line of walking wounded heading toward the finish. There was no joy in advancing my position relative to other runners, but it did offer an opportunity to exchange encouragement and talk. At this point, we weren't racing each other, we were racing against the course.

My brother started firmly encouraging me with smack talk. "You can make it. You are not going to fail. You are going to finish this bitch. You will be an IRONMAN®. Marines don't quit." As the race progressed, his verbal support became louder. Some of this was valuable, but most of it was unfortunately just more input noise to an already overloaded sensory experience.

The later the evening went, the louder he got. At one point I was embarrassed by his chants, but mostly I was glad for his company and that he was my brother. In fact, his encouraging words not only helped get me over the finish line, they also encouraged him and his wife to register for the IRONMAN Wisconsin race in 2012—which they both finished.

Marathon Mile 9— Chicken Soup for the Soul

At about mile nine, there was an aid station that was passing out chicken broth. I was told by many people that this liquid would go down easy, sooth my stomach, and provide the sodium necessary to keep me moving. I grabbed a steaming hot cup from a volunteer and said thank you then stepped to the side of the running path and took a long pull from the styrofoam cup. I slowly swished the broth around in my mouth.

The taste of chicken soup brought back memories of staying home from school sick as a young child, wearing my red fuzzy footy pajamas with downhill skiers on them and playing with my dog. My mom fed us grilled cheese sandwiches, chicken soup, and 7-Up when we were sick. I savored the thoughts and swallowed the soup with a big gulp. The warm liquid flowed down into my stomach and then immediately turned around and rushed back up my throat.

I began vomiting, but kept walking until the chicken broth and everything else was out of my stomach. Once all of the liquid was out, I finished up by dry heaving from deep within my stomach several times. Nobody running past me seemed particularly interested in the fact that I was upchucking. I stopped moving forward and bent over with my hands on my knees. I needed a break. The clock kept tick-tocking. I was wasting time. After a few minutes, the stomach spasms were over. I wiped my chin with the tail of my T-shirt, put my left foot in front of my right, and began running again.

Marathon Mile 13— Halfway

At mile thirteen, the halfway point, slower runners like me turned left around the capitol and headed back out on the second 13.1-mile loop. At the same time, faster runners ran through the turnaround point into the finisher's chute, completing the marathon.

As I headed back out on the second loop, I could see the faster runners finishing the race. This was slightly demoralizing but was also a sign that I only had another half-marathon to go to finish this beast.

As I ran down State Street on the way out of town for the second time that day, I could smell Italian, Greek, and Indonesian food. It made me hungry and nauseous at the same time. Cow bells were screaming. Drunken college students were giving high fives. The next time I set foot on this part of State Street would be the final mile to the finish. My determination to finish was growing stronger with every step.

Thankfully, the dampness of the night was setting in. Volunteers were handing out glow loops for runners to place around their necks as safety devices. I was in a crowd of runners at this point and didn't slow down to grab mine. Soon, the city skyline was behind us as we worked our way back toward the lake and the dark night ahead.

Marathon Mile 15— Sugar Fix

Around mile 15, my daughter Anna showed up. She was waiting all by herself in a dark part of the course. All I could say to her was, "Get me a Fanta orange soda and a Snickers bar." I then took off my hat, long sleeve shirt, and fanny pack and handed them to her in one sweaty lump. She shoved the wet mess into her back pack and took off to get orange pop for her pop. The day's heat had carried into the night and it was still in the mid-seventies.

Marathon Mile 16— Night of the Living Dead

I was mostly walking at this point, and in a moment of irony, I got passed by spectators who were walking along the street going the same direction I was. This embarrassed me into picking up the pace somewhat. At roughly mile 16 there were half a dozen stairs in the middle of the course that I needed to climb. On the third step, my left hamstring locked up and I began to fall backward. I grabbed the handrail tight to keep from falling. My brother Al was right beside me at that point and started pounding my hamstring with his fists in an attempt to loosen them up. I bit my lower lip, flexed my leg a little, and limped up the last two stairs.

It was only ten more miles to the finish, but I would not make it with the extreme muscle cramps I was having. I was determined to finish this beast but somehow needed to pull a rabbit out of a hat to do it. Once again, I went into problem solving mode.

I had already taken as many superman pills as I thought was medically reasonable, so I decided against taking more. I was done drinking sports drink. The amount of time it took for the liquid to go from my lips to my stomach and then back up was only a few seconds, so that didn't seem like a good idea.

I asked my sister Jayne to get some Bengay from the local Walgreens, and off she went. She came back shortly and helped me put the Bengay on my legs. Whew. It seemed to loosen things up. Around this time, a pebble got into my shoe. I knew that if I sat down to untie my shoe, I wouldn't get back up, so I decided to keep on trucking.

A racer passed me going the other way on the outbound portion of the loop. He had a bloody nose and huge back and blue lump on the side of his face. Someone was holding his arm and walking him along the course. He must have either tipped over and hit the ground on the bike or stumbled and fallen on the run. In addition to being injured, he was at least thirty minutes behind me, putting him in jeopardy of being swept from the course for not making minimum pace. We all looked like zombies. It was like the night of the living dead.

Marathon Mile 17

Near mile 17, I saw a woman puking in a trash barrel on the side of the course. I wasn't sure how to help her or what to say, so I ran past her. I would see her later in the medical tent. Around the same time, I went from vomiting whenever I drank or ate to just vomiting every ten minutes no matter what. Finally, when all of the liquid was out of my stomach, I just starting dry heaving.

Oddly enough, this cycle of run a little, puke, run a little, puke, didn't really bother me a whole lot. As an ex-Marine and hard corps beer drinker, I had done my share of puking in the past. The upchucking seemed more like an inconvenience than a showstopper. I kept moving forward in a progressively better mood. Miles were passing, and I was moving closer to the finish. I forced myself to smile, and the smile seemed to put me in an even better mood.

My brother saw a runner on the side of the course who was going to drop from the race. He introduced him to me and we got into a pretty good run/walk rhythm. We ran together for about two miles and then split up. I was picking up my pace and passing other runners. He ended up finishing the race about ten minutes behind me.

By myself again, my mind wandered. The previous winter, I had read a great book by Elie Wiesel called *Night*. The book details the extreme conditions and circumstances of the author's interment in a Nazi concentration camp. He withstood death, torture, hunger, humiliation, and extreme physical pain. At one point, he was forced to march from one concentration camp to another in deep snow without food, winter clothes, or support. People died of starvation along the way. Others were killed by the guards when they could not continue. Thinking about this helped to put my one day voluntary journey into context and made my problems seem really small.

A triathlon veteran once told me that at no time in his race journey did he ever let himself think that he would not finish. He said that if he had allowed himself to think about not finishing, he probably would have dropped from the race.

It is funny that right from the first day of training I gave myself only a 50/50 chance that I would be properly trained and injury-free enough to make it to the starting line, and then only a 50/50 chance that I would finish. I calculated the odds of me finishing then at twenty-five percent. At each point on race day, I brought these odds back up in my head in a weird kind of self talk on how lucky I was to still be in the race.

At this point, I calculated the finishing odds to be ninety-nine percent. I was going to finish the race. I had come too far to quit.

Marathon Mile 19— The Motivational Mile

At about mile 19, the course had set up what they called The Motivational Mile. This consisted of a group of cheerleaders (females this time) and a bumping sound system jamming out dance music. Since it was dark out, they had gigantic diesel generators powering tall portable lights.

It was awesome. Better yet, though, were the hundreds of signs along the road for the next mile. At registration time, each athlete and their supporters had been allowed one two-foot by three-foot cardboard sign and a hand full of markers to write a motivational saying on.

A few of the signs read "Go Mommy" or "Go Daddy Go." One said "Pain is temporary, pride is forever." I remember reading a quote from Isaiah 40:31: "You will run and not grow weary, you will walk and not grow faint." Also, I saw one of my favorite Vince Lombardi quotes: "It's not whether you get knocked down, its whether you get back up." There were literally hundreds of motivational sayings. My sign, of course, had three simple words: "Otter, Eagle, Possum."

We ran along the lake past the last loop in the course and left the park to make the trek back to the capitol and, ultimately, the finish. It was very dark out, and not many spectators or runners were left on the course. The few athletes who were still going were not very talkative. Everyone was conserving energy to get to the finish.

The topic of conversation between the runners at that point was that we were sure we would get to the finish before the cut-off time, even if we walked slowly. I kept moving. The possum strategy was working, and I felt like I owned the night. For the first time that day, I knew I was going to finish the race.

Marathon Mile 20— The Light at the End of the Tunnel

I hit an aid station at about mile 20. The volunteers were still on duty and extremely engaged. I finally had to stop and get the stone out of my shoe. I dropped my tail on the curb and my cramped legs popped straight out. My shoe was leaking blood and pus, as the pebble had cut quite a hole in my foot.

My foot was a pruned up, white, swollen, wet, stinking mess. As I pulled off my sock, my big toenail got caught in the dry-wick material and pulled off. I looked at the toenail for a few seconds and tossed it to the side of the road. I wouldn't need it that night.

It is common for endurance athletes to lose toenails in long-distance training or races. Generally, the athlete's foot swells after a period of time, pressing the toe against the top of the running shoe. When this happens, the consistent rubbing from the foot strikes eventually rubs the nail loose from the toe. In the past, on average, I had lost a nail on each foot each year. My wife paints her nail beds to cover the awkward appearance of a missing nail when wearing sandals.

I tried to dig the pebble out of my flesh but wasn't able to.

It was kind of tucked under a flap of skin, and I just couldn't dislodge it. I screwed around with it for what seemed like five minutes, the whole time watching people who I had worked so hard to pass now passing me back.

I could just barely make out the words "USMC" and "JUDY" on my forearms. The black marker was mostly washed away from the sweat of the day's effort. My determination to finish, though, was still there, just like the legacy my mom and the Marine Corps had left on my life. I remembered something one of my best Marine Corps buddies had said whenever we took the first step into harm's way: "Mother made it, mother fuck it." I whispered this most primeval chant to myself a few times. I wasn't going to get the pebble out of my foot. Fuck it, I was going to move on.

The competitor in me woke up, and I made a promise to myself to pass all of the people who had just passed me. I got my sock on and stood back up. I slowly started moving my stiff legs and tender feet.

If I twisted my foot slightly left and ran with a particular gait, I didn't feel the extreme pain caused by the pebble still underneath the skin. If I walked, I did feel it. So I ran.

My brother and sister were across the street from me at this point, running along the other side. I could see the state capitol building far off in the distance. It was a tiny white speck at the end of a long uphill run. It was the proverbial light at the end of the tunnel. I was going to finish!

Runners were grouping up as we slowed down going up the slight hill, and I was glad to be in the pack with them. We congratulated each other and kept creeping forward. I was running at this point. Painfully slow, but running.

Marathon Mile 23

I hit the second-to-last water stop right by Camp Randall around 10:45 p.m. It was on a long, flat, wide, dark, and empty road. It was blocked off to traffic and filled with IRONMAN® volunteers. There were dozens of tables set up with water and sports drinks. There were sugar cookies, bananas, grapes, oranges, and pretzels. The last table had ice cubes and little sponges. I put a handful of ice cubes in my shorts and a sponge under my hat.

There was a college student in a Captain America costume giving runners high fives. I couldn't believe it. It was almost 11:00 p.m. on a school night—what was this guy doing out here? I made sure to tell the Captain how cool it was that he was still out there. What enthusiasm! He gave me the customary "looking strong" and I gave him the standard thumbs up back. It occurred to me that his enthusiasm was fueled by being so close to watching all these people finish the IRONMAN Wisconsin race. The power and rush of seeing these athletes coming in at the end of the 140.6 miles must have been as big of a thrill for him as it was for us.

At this point, the possum in me was in high gear, moving as fast as a possum in the dark can run. As the minutes passed, I got closer and closer to the finish. It was inevitable now. All I had to do was keep moving and I would beat the clock to the finish.

My brother was right there with me for the last several miles.

He had not run in over ten years, but he probably ran thirteen miles that night. His daughter, Cailey, showed up at mile 23, and we all ran together.

Marathon Mile 25— Let's Do This Again in 2012

At mile 25, I stopped and Cailey took a picture of me standing next to the mile marker. The enormity of the finish was hanging in the air. There was a look of relief on all of the nearby runners' faces. The night air was refreshing and cool. The streets were dark. Since I was not going to win any money for taking first place that day, I decided to take my time on the last mile of the race and chatted with my niece and brother while we walked, ran, and shuffled forward—truly living in the moment.

It was around that point that my brother decided to run the IRONMAN® Wisconsin race in 2012. Here I was falling apart, and he was thinking that he wanted to join the club. What the heck would make someone who had just watched me go through a day of physical and mental torture decide to sign up to do it himself is beyond me. He asked me if I would run it with him, and, in a weak moment, I said yes (now Alan tells the story differently; he says that I asked him to run the IRONMAN Wisconsin race in 2012 on my fiftieth birthday. And he says in a weak moment he said yes!)

Marathon Mile 26.0— The Last Mile

As I came up to the last mile on State Street, my left foot was so sore from the pebble that I could only step on it in a contorted and twisted position. I didn't care. It was on a long list of issues that I would deal with after the race was over. If I had to, I would hop to the finish on one leg. If I couldn't do that, I still had enough time and drive to crawl my way across the line.

I was soaking wet from sweat and water that had been dumped over me. I felt skinny from all of the weight I had lost and had the sensation that I was floating on air rather than running up the hill to the finish.

In a race of this magnitude, the immediate takes precedent over the important. After a race one year ago, my daughter Leah and I drove in a rental car with our seat belts unbuckled and talked for ten minutes about the ordeal that we just finished. The car's buzzer was going off, indicating that we should buckle our seat belts, but neither of us noticed or cared.

This ability to ignore the warnings coming from the dashboard and focus only on moving forward is a key success factor in a runner's brain. Ignore the warnings from the feet about blisters. Don't worry about toe nails rubbing off. Ignore warnings from the legs about shin splints, warnings from the muscles about hamstring cramps, or warnings from the stomach, lungs, head, and brain, and just keep on trucking down the road.

The end justifies the means. There are no medals for those who try and don't finish.

Marathon Mile 26.1

A volunteer approached me about a half mile from the finish
and gave me final instructions about how to go into the finisher's
chute. She jogged alongside me very slowly. She told me to be
sure to smile and not bunch up with other runners when moving
through the chute. She was the first person that night who did
not look at me like she wasn't sure I was going to finish. She said
"when," not "if."

She offered me a cup of chicken soup, but I just smiled and
said no thank you.

I rounded the corner from State Street onto the north side
of the capitol. It was about 11:30 p.m., and the flood lights were
painting the capitol a surreal white color. Moths were circling in
the cones of light. The capitol was huge and imposing against the
quiet dark sky. The streets immediately around the capitol were
nearly empty, as most of the spectators had gone home.

There was a lot of trash on the sidewalks. I remember trying
to kick a can in the street and stumbling on my iron-tight legs.

I have heard surfers talk about being in the green room, a
kind of a nirvana state where time and motion stand still and you
are living totally in the moment. A green room, a white capitol
building, and a yellow brick road to the finish. I was there, I was
in it, and I knew that this was the moment that I had been training for.

I straightened my shirt, pulled my cap tight, dry heaved one last time, and pushed for the finish. My legs had stopped locking up a mile or so ago, and I was moving forward with relative ease. The stone in my shoe continued to burrow an increasingly larger and messier blister that was leaking out red blood onto my white sneakers. My stomach was empty, my head was spinning, and my vision was a blur. In fact, every piece of me hurt, but collectively nothing really felt bad enough to keep me from the goal.

My little sister Amy and cousin Debbie were at the corner to walk me in. Yes, walk. I couldn't run anymore. That phase was over. I knew that I was going to finish in the timeframe and didn't see any need to rush. I got closer with each step. My sister was talking about my mom and how proud she would be to see me finish if she were still alive. My cousin was cracking jokes. I could hear the insane volume of the finish line and turned the next corner to the top of the hill. The volunteers told my family to run ahead and meet me at the finish. They probably didn't have to run too fast.

By now, the pulsing, thumping, and bumping of the music at the finish line was filling the air. It sounded louder than any football game I had ever been to and was especially enormous given the stillness of the night. The ever-present cow bells, the signature sound of the IRONMAN® Wisconsin race, were everywhere. Spectators were screaming and clapping and singing. I was so overwhelmed by the emotion of the moment that I completely forgot the pain of the day. It was as if I was floating above the used-up skeleton of a man running below me.

Marathon Mile 26.2— Arms Raised Over My Head in a V for Victory

I rounded the last corner and looked straight down the final two hundred yards of the course. It was lit up like an airport runway pointed straight into the heart of the night.

Everything in my head went quiet, and I raised my arms up high over my shoulders in a V. I pumped my clenched fists in the air and shouted as loudly as I could. It was damn near done, and all I had to do was get through the chute and across the finish line.

The finisher's chute was crowded with what seemed like a thousand people who had stayed up late into the night to watch the last few people finish the race. I have been told that the best IRONMAN® stories happen at the end of the night, and people were lined up to see these stories reach their conclusions. They filled the bleachers on both sides of the street. They spilled over into the road and were standing front-to-back and shoulder-to-shoulder many rows deep on the sidewalk.

There were huge floodlights turning the night into day.

Moths were circling in the lights. How amazing that all of these people were still awake on a Sunday night to watch the last of the stragglers reach the finish.

I could hear nothing but the pounding of my heart and the pulsing of the blood in my ears. There was a lot of blurry motion around me, as if I was leading the pack in a NASCAR race. In hindsight, I couldn't have been moving faster than four miles per hour, but it was top speed for me at that point.

The Finish—You Are An IRONMAN®!

One of my primary concerns was that I would get to the finish so late that Mike Reilly would have already gone to sleep. That I would just kind of stumble across the line, unceremoniously unannounced. Not the case. I can clearly remember Mike calling out my name and then saying the words that I wanted to hear so badly: "YOU ARE AN IRONMAN!"

I did not drop my arms until I heard the chirp from my timing chip as I crossed the finish line. I trotted a few steps, and my body slowed down the forward motion of the last sixteen-and-a-half hours.

All of my senses came back online at once. I had finished! My legs were wobbly, and as I finally stopped the forward momentum that I had kept for the last 140 miles, my blood pressure and heart rate instantly dropped. I saw a volunteer with an arm full of medals and I bent my head over long enough for her to slip one over my neck.

A friend had told me earlier in the year that there are only two types of people at the end of the race —those who go to the medical tent and those who go to the food tent. I took a few more steps and then blacked out and hit the ground. Two volunteers quickly scrambled in and surrounded me. In triathlon vernacular, these people were called catchers. A catcher's job is to get ahold of the finisher and help him or her make the transition off the course and back into the spectators area.

It seemed like I was out for ten minutes, but after probably only a few seconds I opened first one eye, then the other. The carnival atmosphere of the finisher's chute surrounded me. I looked past the catchers bent over me and saw my daughter Anna standing behind the cattle grates with my nephews and nieces, cheering loudly. The catchers wanted me to get up and walk to the medical tent. I just wanted to lie there.

I reached down and felt the finisher's medal around my chest. The chaos of the moment was overwhelming. I didn't have much mental capacity left. I did, however, have an overwhelming urge to move. I got into a crouch for a few seconds, then rose up onto my feet.

Kathy had finished the race an hour ahead of me and was allowed back in the finishers staging area to help me up off the ground. I was still in somewhat of a haze and soaking wet from sweat, vomit, and snot. I was really glad to see her. I was really glad she finished, too!

A catcher supported me under each arm for a few moments until I was steady enough to stand on my own. I leaned up against a cattle grate and put a grip on the top rung to balance. The autumn night's chill quickly overpowered me. I began to shake and my teeth were chattering.

I wanted to walk on my own, but my wife and a catcher guided me over to the medical tent. The medical facility was pretty huge. It was made up of several tents connected together. There were about thirty folding chairs organized into a waiting room, and I was given a clipboard to fill out my vital information.

The first thing that the med techs did was weigh me in. One-hundred-and-seventy-eight pounds, soaking wet. I had lost an insane 27 pounds in one day. I sat back down and curled up under the thin reflective space blanket that was given to each finisher when he or she crossed the line. The girl I had seen vomiting into a garbage can on State Street was brought in and sat down in a chair near me.

I leaned in to tell her congratulations, but she could not even lift her head to talk to me. She just leaned forward, put her hand gently on my shoulder, and mumbled something. She was as white as a ghost, and her eyelids were only halfway open. Her hand slipped off my shoulder and she kind of slumped back in her chair. Her finisher's medal glistened around her neck.

The doctor came over and sat next to me. He had the clipboard with my stats in his hand. He said that it was late and they were getting ready to shut down the medical tent, so he would just talk to me straight.

He said that if the statistics were right, I had lost over ten percent of my body weight and was severely dehydrated. He said that if it were any other circumstance, I would be hooked up to an IV and sent to the hospital immediately. However, this was impractical, as there was a waiting list for transport and a high charge for the ambulance trip.

He looked at me and said that he told all of the others he had seen that night to just go back to the hotel, drink plenty of fluids, and get some sleep. If I still felt bad in the morning, I should go into the hospital. That was all I needed to hear. I picked up my stuff and walked out the back door of the tent.

Vince Lombardi was quoted as saying that there is nothing better than lying on the field of battle totally exhausted at the end of the day—victorious! I agree.

The Morning After

Kathy finished in pretty good shape and actually chowed down a slice of pizza at the end of the race. She had a blister on her left foot that was so big that it looked like a golf ball. I have never seen anything like it before or since. Somehow, Kathy and I both made it from the hospital tent into her Beamer. Jayne and Mike had picked up our bikes from the transition area and brought them back to the hotel. Anna was waiting patiently for me to check out of the medical tent. It was about 1:30 a.m. when we finally got back to the room. We had been up for almost twenty-four hours.

The first thing I did was dig the pebble out of my foot with a tweezers and a toenail clipper. I put it on the table next to my bed and decided to keep it as a souvenir of the experience. After Kath got out of the shower, I jumped in and washed the day's blood, sweat, and vomit from my body.

I laid down in the bed and tried to sleep but mostly just stared at the ceiling. After a few hours of leg cramps and night sweats, I gave up and logged into my email at around 5:00 a.m. I sent out thank-you noted to my family, friends, coworkers, training partners, and the coaches who had gotten me to the finish. Kathy got up shortly after me and we decided to pack up the hotel room and head back to the Monona Terrace to pick up our dropped race gear and meet the other racers.

I put on my IRONMAN® finisher T-shirt and proudly

looked at myself in the mirror. There were big dark rings under my eyes. My skin was a sickly translucent yellow color. My shoulders were slumped. I had lost two toenails and could only stand on one leg because of the hole the pebble had cut into my foot. My body was so thin that I looked like a skeleton. My arms hung like toothpicks from the sleeves of my finisher's shirt. My biceps were very tight from grabbing the bike handles, making my hands shake like I had a severe hangover. I could hardly recognize the person looking back at me.

My mom was right; this race was tough on people. I thought about stories I had read of POWs in WWII. How they were tortured, how they suffered, and how their bodies were emaciated. Their years of forced pain were many times more extreme than the daylong voluntary ordeal I had just gone through. This realization snapped me back from the momentary pity party my reflection in the mirror had caused.

I dug through my bags and pulled out a tin of Skoal tobacco that I had purchased two days before. When I bought it, I figured that it would either reward me in victory or comfort me in defeat. I cracked open the can with my thumb and packed a pinch of long-cut wintergreen chewing tobacco in my cheek. It stung, as there were sores in my mouth from the trauma of the race. The nicotine instantly flowed into my bloodstream and a relaxed calm washed over me.

I unpacked a huge smile from deep in my heart and hung it on my face. I had to adjust the smile a few times until it felt natural. I scrunched my favorite camouflage baseball cap down on my forehead and slowly walked out of the hotel room. Hell yes it was real. We finished!

Kath and I checked out of the hotel and packed up the car.

We didn't take the usual care to repack all of the triathlon gear. I just piled heaps of wet clothing and miscellaneous hard gear into the back of the Beamer. The soreness in my muscles was greatly overshadowed by the pain in my foot. Each trip from the hotel room to the car got progressively better as the movement loosened up tight muscles and tender feet.

We drove down to the Monona Terrace one last time to pick up our special needs bags and check out of the race. Athletes were milling around. Most everyone was slightly limping, but there was an aura of success or celebration in the air. It felt like New Year's Day.

The IRONMAN® event staff was breaking down the enormous infrastructure that creates the circus-like atmosphere of the IRONMAN race. They were packing it away in trucks like carnies. Moving it on to the next city, I suppose.

We ran into a few people we had met over the last year's training. Everyone had a great story to tell. One of the better ones was from a guy who was so sick of his bike after getting off of it that he had left it in the corral overnight. It ended up in the lost and found. It was not just an ordinary bike, but one that had cost 10,000 dollars.

The Mark of the Beast

The first weekend after we got back home to Minneapolis, Kath and I jumped into the car and headed to downtown St. Paul. I wanted to get the mark of the beast, the IRONMAN® logo, tattooed onto the back of my right calf. Somewhat of a ritual, it is very common to see it tattooed on the calves of finishers' legs. Many times when I go somewhere in shorts, someone recognizes it. It is part of me. I earned it and it belongs there.

As I lay face down on the tattoo artist's table, I had time to reflect on the journey of the previous two years. The buzzing needle stung as it traced the outline of the IRONMAN logo into my skin. Had I learned anything from the past eighteen months? Absolutely. I learned that everything is possible for any person if he or she trains long enough and hard enough. I also learned that regardless of the problem, there is always a solution.

Lastly, I learned that there is no bigger accomplishment than having strong relationships.

The old me had valued accomplishment over all else: family, friends, self, and maybe even soul. Now that I had won my ultimate achievement, the only thing I could do was look back and think about the summer I had lost hanging out with my friends on the boat, spending time with my buddies at the hunting cabin, or grilling burgers with my family on the deck. I had traded relationships for ambition. What a huge mistake.

Would I do it again? No. Without question. Like Marine Corps boot camp, high school, and marriage, some things are best done only once.

Do I regret doing it? No. The experience changed me and I forever will mark time in two periods: before IRONMAN® and after IRONMAN.

My daughter put it best when she said that I like saying that I did an IRONMAN triathlon much better than I actually liked doing an IRONMAN triathlon.

The race certainly made me more confident in my ability to solve tough problems and overcome large obstacles. It also brought Kathy and I much closer together than we have been at any other point in our relationship.

After the outline of the tattoo was traced, the artist changed needles and filled in the red color of the IRONMAN logo. The process was going very quickly. When the tattoo was finished, I began to think that I had one last thing to do before calling my journey complete.

It seemed like it might be a good idea to write a book about the eighteen months of training leading up to the race and the sixteen hours spent executing the race. A few friends had mentioned the idea to me. Maybe it would bring closure to the event.

Dinner and Drinks

Later that week, Kath and I hooked up for dinner with Mike and Samantha, two people we had trained with that summer. As providence would have it, all four of us had finished the race. Each one of us shared our race stories as the wine flowed. While the stories had some similarities, it was for the most part as if we had run four entirely different races.

Kathy's experience was overall very positive, and it seemed like she finished as strong as she had started. Part of her motivation for running the race was to raise money for MS, and she had gathered an astounding $10,000 in donations. She could not wait to take on the next IRONMAN® race.

Mike's experience was also positive, and he had already signed up for the IRONMAN Canada race. Samantha was so excited to have finished the race that she was still wearing her blue competitor's wrist band a week afterward.

I was, of course, happy I had finished, but I was even happier that I would not be doing another race. I had actually just recently broken the news to my brother that I could not commit the time for another IRONMAN event and that he would have to do the 2012 race by himself.

As the night progressed, we talked about how the race had changed us. We all came to the agreement that what we had really done was not just finished a race, but started on the next adventures that would define the rest of our lives.

Back at the Cabin

Six weeks after the race, I had come full circle and was back at the hunting cabin. It was late fall 2010, and the approximately seventy pounds I had lost in the last eighteen months had been slow to come back on. The physical changes in me from the last year presented a problem keeping up with the drinking, wrestling, hard work and cold weather in the north woods. The mental changes I had gone through made me both more focused and happier than ever to be done with the training and back out in the Minnesota wilderness.

The first night at camp was like a scene out of *The Lord of the Flies*, as eight guys who only see each other a few times a year stayed up late and partied down. I binged on just about every kind of liquor I could get my hands on: beer, home-brewed wine, vodka, tequila, and whiskey. A few hours into the deluge, it made sense to smoke cigarettes. The rush of alcohol and tobacco so soon after an IRONMAN® race was welcome at first, and then overwhelming.

Later that night, after the tipping point between "Hell yeah I'll have another beer!" and "No way in hell will I have another beer!" had passed, I stumbled outside. The stars were as big as basketballs, and the smell of the campfire and crisp air of the evening night welcomed me back to the big woods. I thanked God one more time for carrying Kathy and me across the finish line in Madison, climbed the ladder into the cabin's loft and then passed out in my sleeping bag.

The next morning, as breakfast was being made, I couldn't even get up to eat. When I tried to step out of bed, the cabin started spinning and my stomach revolted. Just opening my eyes hurt my brain. I had a severity three hangover, so I just laid in bed, immobilized. A moth fluttered over my head. I took a lot of heat from my friends, but I just could not get out of my sleeping bag.

At 5:30 a.m., the party headed out to hunt with out me. I had never slept in on the opening morning of a deer hunting season before. I was always one of the first guys in the woods, lining up to get the biggest buck. This morning, it didn't seem to matter, maybe because I had already gotten my trophy that year when I crossed the finish line in Madison. Mostly it was because I'd had way too much to drink the night before.

At about 10:00 in the morning I rolled over and thought about my options. It was hard to shoot a deer while laying on my back in the cabin. Even though it was late in the morning, it didn't mean that I was out of the race to get a big buck. I sat up and pulled on my boots.

I climbed down from the loft and walked to my pickup truck to get my equipment. It was unusually warm for the time of year, maybe in the high twenties, and clear. I slipped on my blaze orange overalls and put five shells into my rifle. I inspected the rifle for problems, double checked that the safety was on, made sure my compass was in my pocket and took the first step on the path to my stand for the morning.

My tree stand was about a quarter-mile from the cabin, and I tried to walk as slow as possible so as to not raise my pulse rate and begin to sweat. I had gotten very in touch with my body's cardio system over the last year and knew that by taking a few resting breaths every now and then I could keep my pulse rate low.

There was no snow on the ground and leaves crinkled and branches snapped as I walked. With each turn of the path, I got further from the cabin and closer to my stand. I laid down a scent trail of doe estrus behind me from a little drip bottle I kept in my hand. If heaven was any better than being in the woods that morning, I could not possibly imagine it.

I climbed up in my stand and settled into the environment. There was still a heavy frost on the earth, and my breath steamed as it came out of my mouth. Squirrels were chirping from the trees, and a grouse crossed in front of me on the ground. Leaves were crunching all around me from the little critters scurrying in the woods. Within a few minutes of setting up, I heard a heavy crashing off to my left. It was either a bulldozer pushing down trees or a rutting buck back tracking my scent trail up the same path I just walked in on.

I pulled my buck call out of my pocket and gave a soft grunt. After a few seconds, I heard a strong hard grunt back and then more crashing through the woods. It had to be a buck, and it seemed like he was close to me. My heart rate instantly picked up and my senses shook the haze from the night before and became razor sharp. Time seemed to slow down, and the activity in the woods stopped for a minute as the squirrels and birds turned an ear to the unfolding drama.

I swiveled my body and placed my rifle in a position that would allow me to get a fast shot off. I put my thumb on the rifle's safety in case I needed to quickly flip it off and fire. The buck emerged from the woods in a place I didn't expect and crossed in front of me about a hundred yards out. His pace and angle didn't allow me to get off a safe shot. He looked in my direction and, sensing something wasn't right, spooked. His foot-long white tail flipped up, and he ran a few steps before walking up a hill and disappearing behind some mossy granite rocks. Just as quickly as he had appeared, he was gone from my sight. I wasn't deterred. I began to problem solve.

I gave another soft grunt call. The buck turned around and reemerged on a rock outcropping about 150 yards from my stand. He pawed the ground and sniffed the air. His neck was huge and swollen from the rut. I put down my rifle and raised my binoculars to take a look at him.

His rack wasn't enormous but appeared to be a solid eight points polished clean from fighting other bucks and scraping trees. His body was massive, and he had a scar across his hind quarters which I assumed came from another buck's horns. His breath was steaming as he angrily snorted out. He was aware that there was another presence in the woods and was looking for love, a fight, or both.

Silhouetted against the morning sun, he looked like a demon from hell, ready for battle. He glared in my direction, and his posture indicated that he had mistaken me for a younger buck encroaching on his territory. He started to walk slowly forward and then turned hard left onto the fork in the path that led back to my position.

He stopped and hesitantly stuck his nose in the air again to collect more information about me. The air was thick with the buck lure scent I had spread on the ground and in cotton swabs in the tree limbs. When he wasn't looking, I slowly set down my binoculars. He stamped the ground purposefully and, with a jolt, started moving straight for me.

I couldn't believe my good luck once again that year. God had encouraged mother nature to give me a perfect day and circumstance. Now it was up to me to take advantage of it. I had to snap my rifle up off my lap and get him in my sights before he ran past me yet again. Microseconds seemed like minutes. I forced myself to wait until his head was behind a rock and then shouldered my rifle and flipped off the safety in a single motion. He was at a full trot, coming straight for me. My heart was beating so loud that I thought he would hear it.

It was the moment of truth. I had spent many years preparing for this and had confidence that I was ready. I placed the crosshairs of the rifle scope over his heart. I had a solid quartering shot. I led him a half inch left to compensate for his speed and squeezed the trigger.

The recoil of the rifle jumped the scope and I momentarily lost sight of the buck. With the crack of the rifle, the 7mm bullet left the barrel at over 2000 feet per second and travelled the 100 yards from me to him. The copper jacketed bullet pierced his hide and his heart exploded. He dropped cold, tumbling to a stop. When the scope came back down from the recoil, I saw that the buck had came to rest on the rocks. There was no movement. The background noise from the woods disappeared. It seemed like all of the critters in the forest including me were holding their breath to see what would happen next.

I cranked the bolt action and locked and loaded another round in the chamber in a microsecond, like I had done hundreds of times before. The scope's crosshairs were now focused on his chest; I was ready to take a second shot. My hands were shaking slightly. My breathing started again and was fast and short. The chill in the morning air was gone. After the echo from the crack of the rifle bounced off into the distance, the woods came back to life. A red squirrel barked at me.

I was consumed with the exhilaration of the moment and the gravity of having just slain this majestic beast. I felt like throwing my hands over my head in a V and letting a loud Marine U-Raa fly. But instead, I just savored the moment in silence.

It seemed like it had all happened so fast, but in reality, I had been preparing for this moment for years and just had the strength and good fortune to execute at the right time.

Afterword

It took Kathy and I approximately a year and a half to train for the IRONMAN® Wisconsin race. It took about the same amount of time to write this story. While I will never run another IRON-MAN triathlon, I may write another book.

I drew on a large audience of friends and training partners to help me write and re-write the book into the form it is in today. Writing this book, like training and finishing an IRONMAN race, was truly a communal event that one person—the author or the finisher—should not unfairly take credit for.

One bit of common feedback from friends who have read the draft of the book is that they felt that my wife pressured me into running the race. This is perhaps partially true, I honestly would have dropped from the race at any point in training, and never looked back—and she would have let me.

Whenever she told me to continue she always said take a week off and think about it because she knew how much train-ing we had already put in and for some odd reason, she always thought I would finish.

Before the race, I just never thought that the reward of crossing the finish line was worth the effort and lost time. Af-ter crossing the finish line, all the blood, sweat, and tears of the previous eighteen months seemed like a small price to pay for the experience and title of being an IRONMAN finisher.

Another common thought from friends who read the initial manuscript is that I somehow succeeded to the finish in spite of my best efforts to fail. In many respects, I don't disagree with this statement. Oftentimes, when I should have been training, I slept in, worked on the farm, went into the office or went out drinking. I was never able to fully commit to the lifestyle.

I surely should have put more time into training, bought better gear, and managed my nutrition better. If I had done these things, maybe I would have finished the course in fifteen-and-a-half hours instead of sixteen-and-a-half. The only things that I really had going for me were an ambition to start, determination to make it to the next milestone, the fear of failure, and the strength to finish.

While it is tough to live in a party world and a endurance athlete culture at the same time, I seem to have lived at both ends of the spectrum. I don't think that I am alone in doing this either. Media and social culture seem to paint a person as either a health nut or a party animal. I think you can be both.

Also, I have heard professional athletes on TV say that God was with them when they scored a goal. I have heard several triathletes say that no competitor is an atheist on race day. I can surely say that God had direct involvement in every aspect of me crossing the finish line that day. He delivered the weather, support, and strength to get me through the longest day in my life.

One of the many odd things about endurance sports is that the running ethic seems to catch on among the friends and relatives of the athlete. After the IRONMAN® Wisconsin race my sisters Amy and Jayne, daughters Leah and Anna, and niece Cailey have all completed half-marathons. My nephew Mitch completed a full marathon at age twenty as did my daughter Anna at age nineteen. My brother Alan and sister-in-law Lisa completed the 2012 IRONMAN Wisconsin race. My seventy-four-year-old dad ran a 5k Turkey Trot with all of his grandchildren in 2010 and 2012. Several of my deer hunting friends have dropped weight and have run half-marathons and together we have competed three mud runs in 2012. My wife encouraged four of her neighbor friends to run a woman's triathlon and our lake association began an annual run or walk around our lake.

Finally, if the toughest thing I ever go through is a seventeen-hour race, I will consider myself blessed. It seems like life seems to hand the ordinary person much more difficult challenges.

The family, top left to right: Anna, Leah (holding Emma), and Kathy (holding Rex). Front row: myself with our dog Gary.

The family in Florida.

Left to right: brother-in-law, Mike; Kathy; sisters Jayne and Amy; and Leah enjoying summer on the boat

Top left: checking-in at the IRONMAN®
Wisconsin race on Saturday
Top right: the ego mirror
Above: the swim
Right: the bike
Opposite page top: feeling on top of the
world coming out of the swim
Opposite page bottom: me on the bike
tackling one of many hills

Kathy and I at the deer farm

2010 buck

Up at the cabin, left to right: Wayne, me, Joel, Jordy, and Jason

Kathy and I (left) with Alan and Lisa (right) at check-in to Mermorial Hermann IRONMAN® 70.3® Texas in Galveston 2012

Family Turkey Trot 2012. Left to right: Sam, Alan, Leah (I am behind Leah), Lisa, Mike, Ethan, Kathy, Mitch, Sarah, Jayne, Megan, Liz, Cailey and Amy. Not pictured are Anna, Jacob, and my father.

CPSIA information can be obtained
at www.ICGtesting.com
Printed in the USA
LVOW04s1254291116

514946LV00017B/561/P